MEDITATIONS

Marcus Aurelius

Meditations

*A New Translation, with an Introduction,
by Gregory Hays*

THE MODERN LIBRARY

NEW YORK

LIBRARY OF CONGRESS CATALOGING-IN-PUBLICATION DATA
Marcus Aurelius, Emperor of Rome, 121–180.
[Meditations. English]
Meditations / Marcus Aurelius; translated, and with an introduction, by
Gregory Hays.
p. cm.
ISBN 0-679-64260-9
1. Ethics.   2. Stoics.   3. Life.   I. Hays, Gregory.   II. Title.
B580.H3 M3713 2002
188—dc21   2001057947

Modern Library website address: www.modernlibrary.com

Printed in the United States of America on acid-free paper

2   4   6   8   9   7   5   3   1

CONTENTS

MEDITATIONS

INTRODUCTION

Gregory Hays

MARCUS AURELIUS ANTONINUS

States will never be happy until rulers become philosophers
or philosophers become rulers.

—PLATO, *The Republic*

Marcus Aurelius is said to have been fond of quoting Plato's dictum, and those who have written about him have rarely been able to resist applying it to Marcus himself. And indeed, if we seek Plato's philosopher-king in the flesh we could hardly do better than Marcus, the ruler of the Roman Empire for almost two decades and author of the immortal *Meditations*. Yet the title is one that Marcus himself would surely have rejected. He never thought of himself as a philosopher. He would have claimed to be, at best, a diligent student and a very imperfect practitioner of a philosophy developed by others. As for the imperial throne, that came almost by accident. When Marcus Annius Verus was born, in A.D. 121, bystanders might have predicted a distinguished career in the Senate or the imperial administration. They could hardly have guessed that he was destined for the imperial purple, or seen in their mind's eye the lonely bronze horseman whose upraised hand greets us from the Capitoline hill in Rome across two thousand years.

Marcus sprang from a distinguished enough family. The year of his birth coincided with his grandfather's second tenure of the consulship, in theory Rome's highest office, though now of largely ceremonial importance. And it was to be his grandfather who brought him up, for his father died when he was very young. Marcus makes reference in the *Meditations* to his father's character as he remembered it or heard of it from others, but his knowledge must have been more from stories than from actual memories. Of the remainder of his childhood and his early adolescence we know little more than can be gleaned from the *Meditations*. The biography of him in the so-called *Historia Augusta* (a curious and unreliable work of the late fourth century probably based on a lost series of lives by the third-century biographer Marius Maximus) tells us that he was a serious child, but also that he loved boxing, wrestling, running and falconry, that he was a good ballplayer and that he loved to hunt. None of these are surprising occupations in an upper-class youth.

Book 1 of the *Meditations* offers glimpses of Marcus's schooling, and we can fill out the picture by what is known of upper-class education generally at this period. His first instructors, like the unnamed teacher mentioned in *Meditations* 1.5, were probably slaves, from whom he would have mastered the rudiments of reading and writing. At a later stage he would have been handed over to private tutors to be introduced to literature, especially, no doubt, Vergil's great epic, the *Aeneid*. But literature served only as a preparation for the real goal. This was rhetoric, the key to an active political career under the empire, as it had been under the Republic. Under the supervision of a trained rhetor, Marcus would have begun with short exercises before progressing to full-scale practice declamations in which he would have been asked to defend one side or another in imaginary law cases, or to advise a prominent historical figure at a turning point in his career. (Should Caesar cross the Rubicon? Should Alexander turn back at the Indus? Why or why not?)

Such training was conducted in Greek as well as Latin. Since at least the beginning of the first century B.C. the Roman upper classes had been essentially bilingual, and Marcus's spoken and written Greek would have been as fluent as the French of a nineteenth-century Russian aristocrat or the Chinese of a Heian Japanese courtier. Marcus would have read Homer's *Iliad* and *Odyssey* and the tragedies of Euripides side by side with the *Aeneid,* and studied the speeches of the great Athenian orator Demosthenes as intensively as those of the Roman statesman Cicero. It was Greek writers and artists who constituted the intellectual elite at the capital; when in later life the emperor conversed with his court physician, Galen, he would have done so in the latter's native tongue. Above all, Greek remained overwhelmingly the language of philosophy. In the late Republic and early empire, writers like Lucretius, Cicero and Seneca had worked to create a philosophical literature in Latin, with notable success. But the great thinkers—Plato, Aristotle, Theophrastus, Zeno, Chrysippus, Epicurus, etc.—had all been Greeks. Serious philosophical investigation required a familiarity with the language they wrote in and the terminology they developed. That Marcus composed his own *Meditations* in Greek is natural enough.

In 137, when Marcus was sixteen, a crucial event took place. The reigning emperor, Hadrian, was childless. An illness had brought him near to death a year previously, and it was clear that he would not live forever. Hadrian owed his throne to his adoption by his predecessor and distant relative, Trajan. Following Trajan's example, Hadrian had designated the distinguished aristocrat Lucius Ceionius Commodus to succeed him. In 137, however, Ceionius died unexpectedly, and Hadrian was forced to cast about for a new successor. His choice fell on the childless senator Antoninus, whom he selected with the proviso that Antoninus should in turn adopt Marcus (his nephew by marriage) along with Ceionius's son Lucius Verus, then aged seven. Marcus took on the family name of his adopted father, becoming Marcus Aurelius Antoninus.

Hadrian's death the following year left Marcus first in line for the throne. His education and that of the younger Verus were now matters of still greater concern, and it is clear that no expense was spared. For training in Greek rhetoric, he was entrusted to Herodes Atticus, a fabulously wealthy Athenian rhetorician whose tempestuous relations with his family, fellow citizens and the imperial court itself would have furnished ample material for a soap opera. His instructor in Latin oratory was Marcus Cornelius Fronto, a prominent rhetorician from Cirta in North Africa. By an accident of fate, many of Fronto's letters to Marcus have survived, and they illustrate the close relationship between student and teacher. They also suggest Fronto's regret at seeing Marcus move away from rhetoric to delve ever more deeply into philosophy. The first book of the *Meditations* pays tribute to a number of philosophers from whom Marcus learned, both formally and informally, and he is likely to have studied with or listened to many others.

Marcus would have learned much outside the classroom as well. For training in legal and political matters, an informal apprenticeship bound aristocratic youths to older public figures—men like Junius Rusticus, whose influence Marcus chronicles in 1.7. But the single greatest influence was surely Marcus's adopted father, Antoninus Pius. Marcus would have watched as Antoninus received embassies, tried legal cases and dictated letters to his deputies. Meanwhile Marcus's own position as heir apparent was signaled in various ways. In 140 he served as consul (at the age of nineteen), and would serve again in 145. In the same year he married Antoninus's daughter Faustina, to whom he pays tribute in *Meditations* 1.17.

Edward Gibbon's *History of the Decline and Fall of the Roman Empire* describes the reign of Antoninus as "furnishing very few materials for history, which is indeed little more than the register of the crimes, follies, and misfortunes of mankind." It furnishes equally little material for Marcus's biography. In the decade and a half between 145 and 161 we learn little of Marcus's occupations, and our only glimpses of his inner development come from his correspondence with Fronto. But the two poles that would govern the remainder of his life—the court and philosophy—seem by this point to be fully established. There is no evidence that Marcus experienced anything like the "conversion" to philosophy that some ancient figures experienced (or affected), but it is clear that by the middle to late 140s philosophy was becoming increasingly central to his life.

On August 31, 161, Antoninus died, leaving Marcus as his sole successor. Marcus immediately acted to carry out what appears to have been Hadrian's original intention (perhaps ignored by Antoninus) by pushing through the appointment of his adopted brother, Lucius Verus, as co-regent. Verus's character has suffered by comparison with Marcus's. Ancient sources, in particular the gossipy *Historia Augusta,* tend to paint him as a self-indulgent degenerate—almost another Nero. This may be unfair; it is certainly not the picture of him we get from Marcus's own reminiscences in the *Meditations.* It does seem clear, however, that Marcus functioned as the senior emperor in fact if not name. It would be surprising if he had not. He was almost a decade older, and had been trained for the position by Antoninus himself.

What kind of ruler did this philosopher-king prove to be? Not, perhaps, as different from his predecessors as one might have expected. Though an emperor was all-powerful in theory, his ability to control policy was in reality much more limited. Much of his time was spent fielding problems that had moved up the administrative ladder: receiving embassies from the large cities of the empire, trying appeals of criminal cases, answering queries from provincial governors and dealing with petitions from individuals. Even with a functional system of imperial couriers, news could take weeks to travel from the periphery of the empire to the center; imperial edicts took time to move down the chain of command. While the emperor's decision had the force of law, enforcement was almost entirely in the hands of provincial governors, whose diligence might be affected by incompetence, corruption, or an understandable desire not to antagonize local elites.

We get occasional glimpses of Marcus's day-to-day duties from the evidence of imperial decisions preserved in letters, inscriptions and the legal codes. Surviving legislation shows a certain interest in the freeing of slaves and in regulations relating to the guardianship of orphans. Attempts have been made to tie the first to Marcus's philosophical convictions and the second to his own memories of life without a father. But it remains unclear how much of the policy is due to Marcus himself, and how far it differs from that of Marcus's predecessor, Antoninus. Perhaps more interesting are the traces of Marcus's personality to be discerned in the phrasing of imperial documents, where we find a scrupulous attention to detail and a self-consciousness about linguistic usage that seems to differentiate Marcus from his predecessors. Neither trait surprises in the author of the *Meditations* or a student of Fronto, whose extant letters place great stress on the quest for the *mot juste*.

One of Marcus's priorities was to preserve good relations with the Senate. The goal was to disguise the absoluteness with which the emperor ruled: to preserve a facade—and sometimes, no doubt, even to achieve the reality—of consensus and cooperation. A hundred years before, aristocrats might have dreamed of a restored Republic (as some certainly did). But by the second century it was clear that there was no alternative to the principate. The Senate expected deference in public and hoped for influence behind the scenes; "good" emperors were willing to play along. In cultivating the upper classes Marcus was following in the footsteps of Antoninus and Trajan, rather than of Hadrian, whose relations with the Senate had been prickly. And it is this, as much as anything else, that is responsible for his reputation as a benevolent statesman. An emperor might do as he liked while he lived, but it was the senatorial historians—men like Cornelius Tacitus in the 120s or Cassius Dio in the generation after Marcus's death—who had the last word.

Another area where Marcus's policy continued that of his predecessors related to a small and eccentric sect known as the Christians. In the course of the next century they would become an increasing problem for the imperial administration, and they were prominent enough in Marcus's day to attract an extended denunciation from a certain Celsus, part of whose work "Against the Christians" still survives. The sect met with contempt from those intellectuals who deigned to take notice of it (Marcus's tutor Fronto was evidently one), and with suspicion and hostility from ordinary citizens and administrators. The Christians' disfavor stemmed from their failure to acknowledge the gods worshipped by the community around them. Their "atheism"—their refusal to accept any god but their own—endangered their neighbors as well as themselves, and their reluctance to acknowledge the divine status of the emperor threatened the social order and the well-being of the state.

Christianity had been illegal since the early second century
when a query from Pliny the Younger (then governor of Bithynia
in Asia Minor) prompted the emperor Trajan to establish a formal
policy: While Christians were not to be sought out, those who con-
fessed to the faith were to be executed. But empire-wide persecu-
tion did not become a reality until a much later date. The main
threat to Christians in the second century came from individual
provincial governors, acting either on their own initiative or under
pressure from local communities. In the late 170s, for example, civic
unrest at Lyons resulted in a virtual pogrom of Greek-speaking
Christians resident there. Marcus's mentor Junius Rusticus had tried
and executed Christians (the apologist Justin Martyr among them)
in his capacity as city prefect. Marcus himself was no doubt aware of
Christianity, but there is no reason to think that it bulked large in his
mind. The one direct reference to it in the *Meditations* (11.3) is
almost certainly a later interpolation, and the implicit references
some scholars have discerned are surely illusory.

Marcus, in any case, had more serious concerns than this trou-
blesome cult. Soon after his accession, relations between Rome and
its only rival, the Parthian empire in the East, took a dramatic turn
for the worse. Since at least the time of Trajan the two states had
been locked in a cold war that would continue for the next two centuries, and that once a generation or so flared up into a military
conflict. The death of Antoninus and the accession of two new and
untried rulers may have tempted the Parthian ruler Vologaeses III
to test the waters. In 162 his forces occupied Armenia and wiped
out a Roman garrison that had gone to the rescue. Syria itself was
threatened. Rome had no choice but to respond.

It was Verus, the younger emperor, who was sent east, where he
remained for the next four years. Neither he nor Marcus had any
military experience to speak of (Antoninus's peaceful reign had

given little scope for it), and the day-to-day conduct of the war was no doubt left to the professionals. After initial setbacks the Romans rallied and, under such commanders as the dynamic young Avidius Cassius, forced the Parthians to sue for peace. Parthia would remain a threat, but one that could be dealt with by diplomatic means for the immediate future.

Verus and his senior colleague had no time to bask in their triumph, however. Within a year the empire was in the grip of a devastating plague, apparently brought back from the East by Lucius's troops. Its effects may not have been quite as apocalyptic as later writers suggest, but the death toll was certainly high, and it also delayed the emperors' response to a second threat. This was the increasing instability on the empire's other border, the northern frontier that separated Rome from the barbarian peoples of Germany, eastern Europe and Scandinavia. During this period a number of these tribes were under pressure from peoples farther north and reacted by moving across the empire's borders—not for conquest, but in search of land to settle. Rome's reaction alternated between aggressive resistance and attempts at accommodation; its failure to develop a workable policy would eventually result in the collapse of the Western empire some three centuries later.

In some places a line could be drawn. Hadrian's great wall, stretching across Britain, was intended to secure the empire's most distant frontier; under Antoninus it had been briefly superseded by a second line farther to the north. But such fortifications were impracticable on the continent, and it was there that the threat was concentrated. Rome still remembered the catastrophe of A.D. 9, when the Roman general Varus and three legions had marched into the forests of Germany, never to return. In the second century, the greatest source of anxiety was the area farther south, roughly corresponding to modern-day Romania and Hungary.

Trajan's conquest of Dacia two generations before had cleared out a possible source of trouble, but the potential for friction remained. In Marcus's day three peoples presented a special problem: the Quadi, the Marcomanni, and the Jazyges, also called Sarmatians. The removal of three legions to Parthia had seriously weakened the Roman position on the northern frontier, and barbarians took advantage of the situation. In 168, Marcus and Verus marched north to deal with them.

Much of the remainder of the reign would be spent on intermittent warfare, first in the so-called Marcomannic Wars of the early 170s and then in a second campaign later in that decade. And most of the burden was to be borne by Marcus alone, for Verus died suddenly (apparently of a stroke) in early 169. It was a very different kind of war than the traditional campaign Verus's armies had waged. The conventional military and diplomatic tactics that worked against the Parthians were of limited use here. Instead, the Romans had to negotiate with individual chieftains whose authority was limited and whose reliability was always in doubt. When negotiation failed, the only alternative was a slow and bloody succession of small-scale engagements rather than pitched battles. The progress of the campaign is recorded on the column erected in Rome to commemorate the close of the Marcomannic Wars. In spite of its triumphal purpose, the engraved scenes that spiral around the monument paint a grim picture of brutal fighting, devastation and execution. "Spiders are proud of catching flies," Marcus notes mordantly, "men of catching hares, fish in a net, boars, bears, Sarmatians" (10.10). The gruesome vignette that opens *Meditations* 8.34 ("a severed hand or foot, or a decapitated head") may well reflect Marcus's own experience.

By 175 the Romans seemed to have gained the upper hand. But at this point disturbing news arrived. Avidius Cassius, who had distinguished himself as a general during the Parthian War and who as governor of Syria now served as virtual regent of the Eastern empire, had revolted and declared himself emperor. Some of the Eastern provinces (notably Cappadocia) remained loyal to Marcus, but Cassius was recognized as emperor throughout much of the East, and in particular in Egypt, whose grain supply was crucial to the capital. Civil war seemed inevitable, and was prevented only by Cassius's assassination at the hands of a subordinate. Marcus was nevertheless obliged to travel east to reassert his authority, taking with him Faustina (who died in the course of the journey). He visited the major cities of the East, Antioch and Alexandria, arriving finally at Athens, where he was initiated into the Eleusinian Mysteries, a set of mystic rites connected with the worship of Demeter, the goddess of agriculture.

Now in his fifties, Marcus was in declining health, and the revolt of Cassius had only underlined the need to make arrangements for the succession. Faustina had borne at least thirteen children, many of whom had died young. By the mid-170s, Marcus had only one surviving son, Commodus, just entering his teens. There was no reason for Marcus to continue the policy of adoption followed by his predecessors, and there is no reason to think he even considered it. The years that follow see Commodus's rapid promotion to a position not far short of co-emperor. He was consul in 177 at the age of fifteen. In the same year he was accorded all the major imperial privileges, except for the post of Pontifex Maximus, the head of the Roman state religion, held by the reigning emperor alone, and for life.

The gains of the Marcomannic Wars had not proved permanent, and in 178, Marcus and Commodus marched north again. Two years later Marcus died at age fifty-eight, the first emperor to pass on the throne to his son since Vespasian a century before.

Sadly, Commodus's performance did not bear out whatever promise Marcus had discerned in him. He was to be remembered as a dissolute tyrant, a second Caligula or Nero whose many defects were only emphasized by the contrast with his father. His assassination after a twelve-year reign would usher in the first in a series of power struggles that would burden the empire for the next century.

PHILOSOPHICAL BACKGROUND

The composition of the *Meditations* is normally dated to the 170s—Marcus's last decade. That this was a dark and stressful period for him can hardly be doubted. In the ten years between 169 and 179 he had to cope with constant fighting on the frontier, the abortive revolt of Cassius, and the deaths of his colleague Verus; his wife, Faustina; and others. Though he could hardly have anticipated the century of turmoil that would follow his death, he may have suspected that his son and successor, Commodus, was not the man he hoped. That in these circumstances Marcus should have sought consolation in philosophy is only natural. But understanding what Marcus looked for from his philosophical studies requires a certain amount of orientation. To understand the *Meditations* in context, we must familiarize ourselves not only with Stoicism, the philosophical system that underlies the work, but also with the role of philosophy in ancient life more generally.

Today philosophy is an academic discipline, one that few people other than professional philosophers would consider central to their everyday existence. While we may think of ourselves as having a "philosophy of life," it bears little relation to what goes on in the philosophy departments of our universities. The careers of twentieth-century analytic philosophy often seem remote from what the American philosopher Thomas Nagel terms "mortal questions": the problems involved in making ethical choices, constructing a just society, responding to suffering and loss, and coming to terms with the prospect of death. Indeed, most of us would be inclined to see these issues as the province of religion rather than philosophy.

For Marcus and his contemporaries, the situation was very different. Ancient philosophy certainly had its academic side. Athens and other large cities had publicly financed chairs of philosophy, and professional philosophers taught, argued and wrote, as they do today. But philosophy also had a more practical dimension. It was not merely a subject to write or argue about, but one that was expected to provide a "design for living"—a set of rules to live one's life by. This was a need not met by ancient religion, which privileged ritual over doctrine and provided little in the way of moral and ethical guidelines. Nor did anyone expect it to. That was what philosophy was for.

Philosophy in the modern sense is largely the creation of one man, the fifth-century B.C. Athenian thinker Socrates. But it is primarily in the Hellenistic period that we see the rise of philosophical sects, promulgating coherent "belief systems" that an individual could accept as a whole and which were designed to explain the world in its totality. Of these Hellenistic systems the most important, both for Romans in general and for Marcus in particular, was the Stoic school. The movement takes its name from the stoa ("porch" or "portico") in downtown Athens where its founder, Zeno (332/3–262 B.C.), taught and lectured. Zeno's doctrines were reformulated and developed by his successors, Cleanthes (331–232 B.C.) and Chrysippus (280–c. 206 B.C.). Chrysippus in particular was a voluminous writer, and it was he who laid the foundations for systematic Stoicism. This early "academic" Stoicism is the source of certain key terms and concepts that reappear frequently in the *Meditations,* and proper understanding of Marcus's approach requires some familiarity with the system as a whole.

Stoicism

Of the doctrines central to the Stoic worldview, perhaps the most important is the unwavering conviction that the world is organized in a rational and coherent way. More specifically, it is controlled and directed by an all-pervading force that the Stoics designated by the term *logos.* The term (from which English "logic" and the suffix "-logy" derive) has a semantic range so broad as to be almost untranslatable. At a basic level it designates rational, connected thought—whether envisioned as a characteristic (rationality, the ability to reason) or as the product of that characteristic (an intelligible utterance or a connected discourse). *Logos* operates both in individuals and in the universe as a whole. In individuals it is the faculty of reason. On a cosmic level it is the rational principle that governs the organization of the universe.[1] In this sense it is synonymous with "nature," "Providence," or "God." (When the author of John's Gospel tells us that "the Word"—*logos*—was with God and is to be identified with God, he is borrowing Stoic terminology.)

All events are determined by the *logos,* and follow in an unbreakable chain of cause and effect. Stoicism is thus from the outset a deterministic system that appears to leave no room for human free will or moral responsibility. In reality the Stoics were reluctant to accept such an arrangement, and attempted to get around the difficulty by defining free will as a voluntary accommodation to what is in any case inevitable. According to this theory, man is like a dog tied to a moving wagon. If the dog refuses to run along with the wagon he will be dragged by it, yet the choice remains his: to run or be dragged. In the same way, humans are responsible for their choices and actions, even though these have been anticipated by the *logos* and form part of its plan. Even actions which appear to be—and indeed are—immoral or unjust advance the overall design, which taken as a whole is harmonious and good. They, too, are governed by the *logos.*

But the *logos* is not simply an impersonal power that governs and directs the world. It is also an actual substance that pervades that world, not in a metaphorical sense but in a form as concrete as oxygen or carbon. In its physical embodiment, the *logos* exists as *pneuma*, a substance imagined by the earliest Stoics as pure fire, and by Chrysippus as a mixture of fire and air. *Pneuma* is the power—the vital breath—that animates animals and humans. It is, in Dylan Thomas's phrase, "the force that through the green fuse drives the flower," and is present even in lifeless materials like stone or metal as the energy that holds the object together—the internal tension that makes a stone a stone. All objects are thus a compound of lifeless substance and vital force. When Marcus refers, as he does on a number of occasions, to "cause and material" he means the two elements of these compounds—inert substance and animating *pneuma*—which are united so long as the object itself exists. When the object perishes, the *pneuma* that animated it is reabsorbed into the *logos* as a whole. This process of destruction and reintegration happens to individual objects at every moment. It also happens on a larger scale to the entire universe, which at vast intervals is entirely consumed by fire (a process known as *ekpyrosis*), and then regenerated.[2]

If the world is indeed orderly, if the *logos* controls all things, then the order it produces should be discernible in all aspects of it. That supposition not only led the Stoics to speculate about the nature of the physical world but also motivated them to seek the rationality characteristic of the *logos* in other areas, notably in formal logic and the nature and structure of language (their interest in etymology is reflected in several entries in the *Meditations*). This systematizing impulse reappears in many other fields as well. The catalogue of Chrysippus's own works preserved by the late-third-century biographer Diogenes Laertius is very long indeed; it includes not only philosophical treatises in a narrow sense, but also works such as "On How to Read Poetry" and "Against the Touching Up of Paintings." Later Stoics would try their hands at history and anthropology as well as more conventionally philosophical topics.

The expansion of Stoic thought was not only intellectual but also geographical. The movement had been born in Athens. In the century and a half that followed Chrysippus's death it spread to other centers, in particular to Rome. The Romans of the second century B.C. were in the midst of a course of conquest that by the end of the century would leave them the effective masters of the Mediterranean. With conquest came culture. Looking back on the rapid Hellenization of the Roman aristocracy between 200 B.C. and his own day, the poet Horace famously observed that "conquered Greece was the true conqueror." Nowhere is the influence of Greece more obvious than in philosophy. Greek philosophers, including the Stoics, Panaetius (c. 185–109 B.C.), and Posidonius (c. 135–50 B.C.), visited Rome to lecture. Many spent extended periods there. In the first century B.C. it became the fashion for young upper-class Romans to study in Athens, in an ancient version of the eighteenth-century Grand Tour. Roman aristocrats acted as patrons to individual philosophers and assembled large libraries of philosophical texts (like that at the famous Villa of the Papyri at Herculaneum), and Romans like Cicero and Lucretius attempted to expound Greek philosophical doctrines in Latin.

Of the major philosophical schools, it was Stoicism that had the greatest appeal. Unlike some other sects, the Stoics had always approved of participation in public life, and this stand struck a chord with the Roman aristocracy, whose code of values placed a premium on political and military activity. Stoicism has even been described, not altogether unfairly, as the real religion of upper-class Romans. In the process it became a rather different version of the philosophy from that taught by Zeno and Chrysippus. Perhaps the most important development was a shift in emphasis, a narrowing of focus. Early and middle Stoicism was a holistic system. It aimed to embrace all knowledge, and its focus was speculative and theoretical. Roman Stoicism, by contrast, was a practical discipline—not an abstract system of thought, but an attitude to life. Partly for historical reasons, it is this Romanized Stoicism that has most influenced later generations. Indeed, the application of the adjective "stoic" to a person who shows strength and courage in misfortune probably owes more to the aristocratic Roman value system than it does to Greek philosophers.

Stoicism in its later form was a system inspired as much by individuals as by texts or doctrines. One of its most distinguished adherents was Marcus Cato (known as Cato the Younger to distinguish him from his great-grandfather, prominent a century earlier). A senator of renowned rectitude when Julius Caesar marched on Rome in 49 B.C., Cato sided with Caesar's rival Pompey in defense of the legitimate government. When it was clear that Caesar would triumph, Cato chose not to survive the Republic, killing himself after the battle of Munda in 46. Within a century he had become an emblem of Stoic resistance to tyranny. Under Nero he was immortalized by the poet Lucan and praised in a laudatory biography by the senator Thrasea Paetus, whose own resistance to Nero cost him his life. Thrasea's son-in-law, Helvidius Priscus, played a similar role—and came to a similar end—under Vespasian. Thrasea and Helvidius in their turn served as role models to second-century aristocrats like Marcus's mentors Rusticus, Maximus, and Severus. Marcus himself pays tribute to them (and to Cato) in *Meditations* 1.14.

Cato, Thrasea, and Helvidius were doers, not writers, and their legendary heroism inevitably lends them a somewhat two-dimensional quality. A more complex and much more interesting figure was the poet Lucan's uncle, Lucius Annaeus Seneca (c. 4 B.C.–A.D. 65), commonly known as Seneca the Younger to distinguish him from his equally distinguished father. Originally councillor to the young Nero, he was eventually forced to commit suicide after being implicated in an attempted coup against his erstwhile pupil. Men's lives are not always consistent with their ideals, and some critics have found it hard to reconcile Seneca's fabulous wealth and his shameless flattery of Nero with his philosophical views. Yet his works (in particular the *Letters to Lucilius*) remain the most engaging and accessible expressions of later Stoicism. Because they were written in Latin they were also among the most influential on succeeding generations.

But not all Stoics were wealthy senators. There was another kind of Stoic exemplar as well: the outsider whose ascetic lifestyle won him the admiration of his wealthier contemporaries and enabled him to criticize the pretenses of upper-class society with real authority. An early example of the type is Gaius Musonius Rufus (c. 30–100), a member of the Roman administrative class, the so-called knights (*equites*), who was banished by both Nero and Vespasian. A still more dramatic example was Musonius's student Epictetus (c. 55–c. 135), who had taken up the practice of philosophy as a slave and devoted the remainder of his life to it after being freed. He had been exiled to Nicopolis (in northern Greece) under Domitian, and after the tyrant's death, elected to remain there where he taught and lectured to visitors who often traveled great distances to study with him.

One of these was the upper-class historian and statesman Arrian (c. 86–160), who published an extensive record of the master's discussions, a text conventionally referred to as the *Discourses of Epictetus.* He later produced an abridged version, the *Encheiridion* ("Manual" or "Handbook"). Epictetus seems to have been an especially important figure for Marcus. He thanks his philosophical mentor Rusticus for introducing him to "Epictetus's lectures" (either the *Discourses* themselves or a private set of lecture notes), and a series of quotations and paraphrases from the philosopher appear in Book 11 of the *Meditations.* And Arrian's abridged *Encheiridion* provides the closest literary parallel to the *Meditations* itself, not only in its content, but also in its form: a series of relatively short and unrelated entries.

Stoicism and the Meditations

The late Stoicism of Epictetus is a radically stripped-down version of its Hellenistic predecessor, a philosophy which "had learnt much from its competitors and had almost forgotten parts of itself."[3] Both these tendencies, the narrowing of the field and the eclectic borrowing from non-Stoic sources, can be discerned also in the *Meditations.*

Chrysippus and his followers had divided knowledge into three areas: logic, physics and ethics, concerned, respectively, with the nature of knowledge, the structure of the physical world and the proper role of human beings in that world. Marcus pays lip service to this triadic division in at least one entry (8.13), but it is clear from other chapters and from the *Meditations* as a whole that logic and physics were not his focus. Among the things for which he thanks the gods is that he was never "absorbed by logic-chopping, or preoccupied by physics" (1.17). Occasional entries show an awareness of Stoic thought about language (the etymological pun in 8.57 is perhaps the clearest example), but they are the exception, not the rule. In many cases Marcus's logic is weak—the logic of the rhetorician, not of the philosopher; it is rare to find a developed chain of reasoning like that in *Meditations* 4.4. His interest in the nature of the physical world is limited to its relevance to human problems. About one of the basic Stoic physical doctrines—the notion of the periodic conflagration (*ekpyrosis*) that ends a cosmic cycle—Marcus adopts an agnostic position (though he was not alone in this). To him it was ethics that was the basis of the system: "just because you've abandoned your hopes of becoming a great thinker or scientist, don't give up on attaining freedom, achieving humility, serving others..." (7.67).

The questions that the *Meditations* tries to answer are primarily metaphysical and ethical ones: Why are we here? How should we live our lives? How can we ensure that we do what is right? How can we protect ourselves against the stresses and pressures of daily life? How should we deal with pain and misfortune? How can we live with the knowledge that someday we will no longer exist? It would be both pointless and impertinent to try to summarize Marcus's responses; the influence of the *Meditations* on later readers springs in part from the clarity and insistence with which he addresses these questions. It may be worthwhile, however, to draw attention to one pattern of thought that is central to the philosophy of the *Meditations* (as well as to Epictetus), and that has been identified and documented in detail by Pierre Hadot. This is the doctrine of the three "disciplines": the disciplines of perception, of action and of the will.

The discipline of perception requires that we maintain absolute objectivity of thought: that we see things dispassionately for what they are. Proper understanding of this point requires a brief introduction to the Stoic theory of cognition. We have seen that for the Stoics universal order is represented by the *logos*. The *logos* infuses and is wielded by our *hegemonikon* (literally, "that which guides"), which is the intellective part of our consciousness. In different contexts it can approximate either "will" or "character" and it performs many of the functions that English speakers attribute to the brain or the heart.[4] One of its primary functions is to process and assess the data we receive from our senses. At every instant the objects and events in the world around us bombard us with impressions. As they do so they produce a *phantasia*, a mental impression. From this the mind generates a perception (*hypolepsis*), which might best be compared to a print made from a photographic negative. Ideally this print will be an accurate and faithful representation of the original. But it may not be. It may be blurred, or it may include shadow images that distort or obscure the original.

Chief among these are inappropriate value judgments: the designation as "good" or "evil" of things that in fact are neither good nor evil. For example, my impression that my house has just burned down is simply that—an impression or report conveyed to me by my senses about an event in the outside world. By contrast, my perception that my house has burned down and I have thereby suffered a terrible tragedy includes not only an impression, but also an interpretation imposed upon that initial impression by my powers of *hypolepsis*. It is by no means the only possible interpretation, and I am not obliged to accept it. I may be a good deal better off if I decline to do so. It is, in other words, not objects and events but the interpretations we place on them that are the problem. Our duty is therefore to exercise stringent control over the faculty of perception, with the aim of protecting our mind from error.

The second discipline, that of action, relates to our relationship with other people. Human beings, for Marcus as for the Stoics generally, are social animals, a point he makes often (e.g., 5.16, 8.59, 9.1). All human beings possess not only a share of the *logos* but also the ability to use it (that is what makes us human and distinguishes us from other animals). But it would perhaps be more accurate to say that we are *participants* in the *logos*, which is as much a process as a substance. Marcus himself more than once compares the world ruled by *logos* to a city in which all human beings are citizens, with all the duties inherent in citizenship. As human beings we are part of nature, and our duty is to accommodate ourselves to its demands and requirements—"to live as nature requires," as Marcus often puts it. To do this we must make proper use of the *logos* we have been allotted, and perform as best we can the functions assigned us in the master plan of the larger, cosmic *logos*, of which it is a part. This requires not merely passive acquiescence in what happens, but active cooperation with the world, with fate and, above all, with other human beings. We were made, Marcus tells us over and over, not for ourselves but for others, and our nature is fundamentally unselfish. In our relationships with others we must work for their collective good, while treating them justly and fairly as individuals.

Marcus never defines what he means by justice, and it is important to recognize what the term implies and what it does not. All human beings have a share of the *logos*, and all have roles to play in the vast design that is the world. But this is not to say that all humans are equal or that the roles they are assigned are interchangeable. Marcus, like most of his contemporaries, took it for granted that human society was hierarchical, and this is borne out by the images he uses to describe it. Human society is a single organism, like an individual human body or a tree. But the trunk of the tree is not to be confused with the leaves, or the hands and feet with the head. Our duty to act justly does not mean that we must treat others as our equals; it means that we must treat them as they deserve. And their deserts are determined in part by their position in the hierarchy. Stoicism's emphasis on the orderliness of the universe implies a similar orderliness and harmony in its parts, and part of its appeal to upper-class Romans may have been that it did not force its adherents to ask difficult questions about the organization of the society they lived in.[5]

The third discipline, the discipline of will, is in a sense the counterpart to the second, the discipline of action. The latter governs our approach to the things in our control, those that we do; the discipline of will governs our attitude to things that are *not* within our control, those that we have done *to* us (by others or by nature). We control our own actions and are responsible for them. If we act wrongly, then we have done serious harm to ourselves (though not, it should be emphasized, to others, or to the *logos*). By contrast, things outside our control have no ability to harm us. Acts of wrongdoing by a human agent (torture, theft, or other crimes) harm the agent, not the victim. Acts of nature such as fire, illness, or death can harm us only if we choose to see them as harmful. When we do so, we question the benevolence and providence of the *logos,* and thereby degrade our own *logos.*

This, of course, we must not do. Instead we must see things for what they are (here the discipline of perception is relevant) and accept them, by exercising the discipline of will, or what Epictetus calls (in a phrase quoted by Marcus) "the art of acquiescence." For if we recognize that all events have been foreseen by the *logos* and form part of its plan, and that the plan in question is unfailingly good (as it must be), then it follows that we must accept whatever fate has in store for us, however unpleasant it may appear, trusting that, in Alexander Pope's phrase, "whatever is, is right." This applies to all obstacles and (apparent) misfortunes, and in particular to death—a process that we cannot prevent, which therefore does not harm us, and which accordingly we must accept willingly as natural and proper.

Together, the three disciplines constitute a comprehensive approach to life, and in various combinations and reformulations they underlie a large number of the entries in the *Meditations.* We see them laid out starkly and explicitly in *Meditations* 7.54:

> Everywhere, at each moment, you have the option:
> • to accept this event with humility [will];
> • to treat this person as he should be treated [action];
> • to approach this thought with care, so that nothing irrational creeps in [perception].

We find the same triad rephrased and reordered in *Meditations* 9.6: "Objective judgment... Unselfish action... Willing acceptance... of all external events."

And we find it in a more subtle form underlying *Meditations* 8.7:

> ... progress for a rational mind means not accepting falsehood or uncertainty in its perceptions, making unselfish actions its only aim, seeking and shunning only the things it has control over, embracing what nature demands of it—the nature in which it participates, as the leaf's nature does in the tree's.

A score of other entries could be cited. The almost obsessive repetition of these three points suggests that they lie at the very heart of Marcus's thought, and of his project in the *Meditations.*

Other Influences

Marcus Aurelius is often thought of and referred to as the quintessential Stoic. Yet the only explicit reference to Stoicism in the *Meditations* (5.10) is phrased in curiously distant terms, as if it were merely one school among others. The great figures of early Stoicism are conspicuous by their absence. Neither Zeno nor Cleanthes is mentioned in the *Meditations,* and Chrysippus appears only twice—quoted once in passing for a pithy comparison (6.42) and included with Socrates and Epictetus in a list of dead thinkers (7.19). This is not to deny the essentially Stoic basis of Marcus's thought, or the deep influence on him exercised by later Stoic thinkers (most obviously Epictetus). If he had to be identified with a particular school, that is surely the one he would have chosen. Yet I suspect that if asked what it was that he studied, his answer would have been not "Stoicism" but simply "philosophy."

There is nothing surprising about this. The imperial period saw the development of a widespread ecumenical tendency in philosophy. Adherents of most of the major schools—the Platonists, Peripatetics, Cynics, and Stoics—preferred to focus on the points they shared, rather than those that separated them. Not all the figures Marcus credits as influential on his own philosophical development were Stoics; Severus, for example, was a Peripatetic. Although authors like Seneca and Epictetus accepted the basic premises of the system developed by Zeno and Chrysippus, they showed no reluctance to borrow aphorisms, anecdotes, and argumentative strategies from non-Stoic sources. The *Meditations* follows a similar procedure. While built on a Stoic foundation, it also refers to and quotes a wide range of figures, both precursors of the Stoics and representatives of rival schools.

Of the predecessors Marcus invokes, the most important is surely Socrates, the great Athenian thinker who had helped redirect philosophy from a preoccupation with the physical world to a focus on the role of man in society and the nature of human morality. Socrates himself wrote nothing. His teachings were transmitted (and greatly elaborated) in the philosophical dialogues of his student Plato. Marcus quotes Plato repeatedly (especially in Book 7), and Socratic or Platonic elements can be discerned elsewhere too. One example is the so-called Socratic paradox, the claim that no one does wrong willingly, and that if men were able to recognize what is right, they would inevitably do it. "They are like this," Marcus says of other people, "because they can't tell good from evil" (2.1), and he repeats this assertion elsewhere.

Socrates' character was as important as his doctrines. His legendary endurance and self-denial made him an ideal model for the Stoic philosopher—or any philosopher. His refusal to compromise his philosophical beliefs led him to make the ultimate sacrifice when he was put on trial at the age of seventy on trumped-up charges of impiety. His display of integrity at the trial and his comportment in the days leading up to his execution made it easy to view him as a forerunner of first-century Stoic martyrs like Thrasea Paetus or Helvidius Priscus, and it is in this light that Marcus evokes him in *Meditations* 7.66.

Of Socrates' predecessors (the so-called pre-Socratic thinkers), the most important, both for Marcus and the Stoics generally, was Heraclitus, the mysterious figure from Ephesus (in modern-day Turkey) whose Zenlike aphorisms were proverbial for their profundity and obscurity alike. Heraclitus's philosophical system ascribed a central role to *logos* and to fire as the primordial element. Both elements were naturally congenial to the Stoics, and may well have influenced them. Heraclitus is mentioned in a handful of entries in the *Meditations* (4.46, 6.47), but his doctrines can be traced in many others. Moreover, his concision and epigrammatic phrasing anticipate the kind of enigmatic apothegm we find in a number of entries:

The best revenge is not to be like that. (6.6)
Straight, not straightened. (7.12)

The fencer's weapon is picked up and put down again. The boxer's
   is part of him. (12.9)

It is from Heraclitus that Marcus derives one of his most memo-
rable motifs, that of the unstable flux of time and matter in which
we move. "We cannot step twice into the same river," Heraclitus
had said, and we see Marcus expanding on the observation: "Time
is a river, a violent current of events, glimpsed once and already
carried past us, and another follows and is gone" (4.43; and compare
2.17, 6.15).

   Though Heraclitus was clearly the pre-Socratic who most
influenced Marcus, other thinkers leave traces as well. Marcus
twice borrows the poet Empedocles' image of the self-contained
soul as a perfect sphere (8.41, 12.3), and he alludes once to the mystic doctrines of the Pythagoreans (11.27). Several entries explore
the implications of phrases attributed to Democritus, one of the
inventors of the theory of atoms, which would later inspire the
Hellenistic philosopher Epicurus.

   Neither Heraclitus nor Socrates had founded a school. That
was an achievement reserved for Plato, and then for Plato's student
Aristotle, who broke from his master to found the Peripatetic
movement. Marcus never refers to Aristotle, though he does quote
approvingly from the latter's successor Theophrastus (2.10). Probably more important was another fourth-century B.C. movement:
Cynicism. The Cynics, of whom the first and most notorious was
the irascible Diogenes of Sinope, were united less by doctrine than
by a common attitude, namely their contempt for societal institutions and a desire for a life more in accord with nature. Diogenes
himself was largely responsible for the image of a philosopher as
an impoverished ascetic (the "philosopher without clothes" evoked
by Marcus at *Meditations* 4.30 might well be a Cynic). His famous

claim to be a "citizen of the world" surely anticipates, if it did not actually influence, the Stoic conception of the world as a city-state. Marcus refers to Diogenes in several passages, as well as to the latter's student Monimus (2.15), and invokes another Cynic, Crates, at *Meditations* 6.13, in an anecdote whose tenor is now uncertain.

Marcus's relationship to Epicureanism, Stoicism's great rival among Hellenistic philosophical systems, is much more vexed. The followers of Epicurus (341–270 B.C.) believed in a universe radically unlike that posited by Zeno and Chrysippus. The Stoic world is ordered to the nth degree; the Epicurean universe is random, the product of the haphazard conjunctions of billions of atoms. To speak of Providence in such a world is transparently absurd, and while Epicurus acknowledged the existence of gods, he denied that they took any interest in human life. As for humans, our role is simply to live as best we can, making the most of what pleasures are available to us and insulating ourselves as far as possible from pain and anxiety. In particular, we are to feel no anxiety about death, which consists simply in the dissolution of our component atoms. This process is not only inevitable, but harmless, for the simple reason that after death there is no "us" to suffer harm.

Although the sect numbered not a few prominent Romans among its adherents, it never attained the success of Stoicism, and was regarded with genial contempt by most outsiders. The quietism endorsed by the Epicureans was obviously difficult to reconcile with an active public life—an important Roman value—and the Epicurean equation of the good with pleasure was bound to raise eyebrows among conservative Romans. "Eat, drink and be merry" was popularly supposed to be the Epicureans' motto, though Epicurus himself had been quite explicit in identifying pleasure with intellectual contemplation rather than the vulgar enjoyment of food and sex. Though a minority view, Epicureanism was, nonetheless, the only potential rival to Stoicism in offering a systematic cosmology, as Marcus acknowledges on a number of occasions by the stark dichotomy "Providence or atoms" (4.3, 10.6, 11.18, 12.14).

Marcus normally seems to view Epicureanism with disapproval (as we would expect). In *Meditations* 6.10 he contrasts the Epicurean universe, founded on "mixture, interaction, dispersal" with the components of the Stoic system: "unity, order, design"—clearly to the advantage of the latter. Should we not be ashamed to fear death, he asks in another entry, when "even" the Epicureans disdain it? (12.34). But other entries suggest a less dismissive attitude. Marcus quotes with apparent approval Epicurus's account of his own exemplary conduct during an illness (9.41) and twice seeks comfort in the philosopher's remarks on the endurance of pain (7.33, 7.64). Like other late Stoics (Seneca is a notable example), he was willing to accept truth wherever he found it.

Thus far we have been concerned with the content of the *Meditations:* the ethical doctrine of late Stoicism, incorporating a certain amount of Platonic and Heraclitean material, and overlaid with occasional reference to other schools and thinkers. But what of the *Meditations* itself? How and why was it written? Who is its audience? What kind of book is it? For the answers to these questions we must turn from the book's content to its form and origins.

THE *MEDITATIONS:* GENRE, STRUCTURE, AND STYLE

I suspect that Marcus would have been surprised (and perhaps rather dismayed) to find himself enshrined in the Modern Library of the World's Best Books. He would have been surprised, to begin with, by the title of the work ascribed to him. The long-established English title *Meditations* is not only not original, but positively misleading, lending a spurious air of resonance and authority quite alien to the haphazard set of notes that constitute the book. In the lost Greek manuscript used for the first printed edition—itself many generations removed from Marcus's original—the work was entitled "To Himself" (*Eis heauton*). This is no more likely than *Meditations* to be the original title, though it is at least a somewhat more accurate description of the work.[6]

In fact, it seems unlikely that Marcus himself gave the work any title at all, for the simple reason that he did not think of it as an organic whole in the first place. Not only was it not written for publication, but Marcus clearly had no expectation that anyone but himself would ever read it. The entries include a number of cryptic references to persons or events that an ancient reader would have found as unintelligible as we do. While a contemporary might have recognized some of the figures mentioned in *Meditations* 8.25 or 12.27, for example, no ancient reader could have known what was in the letter that Rusticus wrote from Sinuessa (1.7), what Antoninus said to the customs agent at Tusculum (1.16), or what happened to Marcus at Caieta (1.17). Elsewhere Marcus reflects directly on his role as emperor, in terms that would be quite irrelevant to anyone else. We find him worrying about the dangers of becoming "imperialized" (6.30), reminding himself to speak simply in the Senate (8.30), and reflecting on the unique position he occupies (11.7). From these entries and others it seems clear that the "you" of the text is not a generic "you," but the emperor himself. "When you look at yourself, see any of the emperors" (10.31).

How are we to categorize the *Meditations*? It is not a diary, at least in the conventional sense. The entries contain little or nothing related to Marcus's day-to-day life: few names, no dates and, with two exceptions, no places. It also lacks the sense of audience—the reader over one's shoulder—that tends to characterize even the most secretive diarist. Some scholars have seen it as the basis for an unwritten larger treatise, like Pascal's *Pensées* or the notebooks of Joseph Joubert. Yet the notes are too repetitive and, in a philosophical sense, too elementary for that. The entries perhaps bear a somewhat closer resemblance to the working notes of a practicing philosopher: Wittgenstein's *Zettel,* say, or the *Cahiers* of Simone Weil. Yet here, too, there is a significant difference. The *Meditations* is not tentative and exploratory, like the notes of Wittgenstein or Weil, and it contains little or nothing that is original. It suggests not a mind recording new perceptions or experimenting with new arguments, but one obsessively repeating and reframing ideas long familiar but imperfectly absorbed.

Perhaps the best description of the entries is that suggested by the French scholar Pierre Hadot. They are "spiritual exercises" composed to provide a momentary stay against the stress and confusion of everyday life: a self-help book in the most literal sense. A revealing comment in this context is *Meditations* 5.9, where Marcus reminds himself "not to think of philosophy as your instructor, but as the sponge and egg white that relieve ophthalmia—as a soothing ointment." On this reading, the individual entries were composed not as a record of Marcus's thoughts or to enlighten others, but for his own use, as a means of practicing and reinforcing his own philosophical convictions. Such an interpretation accounts for several aspects of the entries that would otherwise be puzzling. It explains the predominance of the imperative in the text; its purpose is not to describe or reflect (let alone to "meditate"), but to urge, direct, and exhort.[7] And it explains also the repetitiveness that strikes any reader of the work almost immediately—the continual circling back to the same few problems. The entries do not present new answers or novel solutions to these problems, but only familiar answers reframed. It was precisely this process of reframing and reexpressing that Marcus found helpful.

The recognition that the entries are as much process as product also accounts for the shapelessness and apparent disorder of the work. We do not know by whom or on what basis the individual books of the *Meditations* were arranged; the order may be chronological, or partly chronological, or wholly arbitrary. The arrangement of the individual entries may or may not be Marcus's own, though its very randomness suggests that it goes back to the author (a later editor would have been tempted to group together thematically similar entries, and perhaps to tie up some of the more obvious loose ends). Nor can we always be sure where individual entries begin and end; in some cases this is a question Marcus himself might not have been able to answer.[8]

A special position is occupied by Book 1, which is distinguished from the rest of the work by its autobiographical nature and by the greater impression of conscious design and ordering apparent in it. It consists of seventeen entries in which Marcus reflects on what he learned from various individuals in his life, either directly or from their example (hence the title I have given the section here, "Debts and Lessons," which has no warrant in the transmitted text). The entries roughly mirror the chronology of Marcus's early life, from his older relatives to his teachers to his adopted father, Antoninus, and ultimately to the gods.[9] This logical schema, as well as the increasing length of the entries, suggests deliberate arrangement, presumably by Marcus himself. If so, then this book, at least, was conceived as an organic whole. It may be among the latest portions of the text, if scholars are correct in thinking (as most do) that the short sketch of Antoninus Pius in *Meditations* 6.30 was the starting point for the longer memoir in 1.16.

Attempts to find organic unity in the remaining books or development from book to book are doomed to failure. Wherever one opens the *Meditations* (with the exception of Book 1) we find the same voice, the same themes; Marcus's thought does not change or develop noticeably from one book to another. Nor can any structure or unity be discerned within individual books. It seems most likely that the division between books is a purely physical one. The transmitted "books," in other words, represent the individual papyrus rolls of Marcus's original, or perhaps of a later copy. When one had been filled, another was begun.[10]

If the books as a whole are homogenous, the individual entries show considerable formal variety. Some are developed short essays that make a single philosophical point; many of the entries in Books 2 and 3 are of this type. Others are straightforward imperatives ("Take the shortest route...") or aphorisms ("no one can keep you from living in harmony with yourself"). Sometimes Marcus will list a number of basic principles in catalogue format ("remember that... and that... and that..."). Elsewhere he puts forward an analogy, sometimes with the point of comparison left to be inferred. Thus human lives are like "many lumps of incense on the same altar" (4.15) or like "a rock thrown in the air" (9.17). In other cases the analogy will be made explicit: "Have you ever seen a severed hand or foot...? That's what we do to ourselves... when we rebel against what happens to us" (8.34). Others present a kind of formal meditative exercise, as when Marcus instructs himself to imagine the age of Vespasian (4.32) or Augustus's court (8.31) and then to compare the imagined scene with that of his own time. Portions of two books (7 and 11) consist simply of quotations. Some entries appear to be rough drafts for others; several of the raw quotations from tragedies in Book 7 are incorporated in the much more polished *Meditations* 11.6. The significance of some entries remains completely obscure. Few critics have known what to make of notes like "Character: dark, womanish, obstinate" (4.28) or "They don't realize how much is included in *stealing, sowing, buying…*" (3.15).

The entries also differ considerably in the degree of artistry they display. Some entries are little more than Marcus's notes or reminders to himself—the philosophical equivalent of "Phone Dr. re appt. Tues.?" But others are highly literary. Marcus wrote as a man trained in the rhetorical techniques of the second century. His thoughts naturally took on the impress of his training and intellectual milieu even when he was writing for himself alone.

The shorter entries often display an interest in wordplay and a striving for epigrammatic brevity that recalls both the ingenuity of the rhetorical schools and the paradoxical compression of Heraclitus:

> Does the sun try to do the rain's work? Or Asclepius Demeter's?
>   (6.43)
> Evil: the same old thing. (7.1)
> Not a dancer but a wrestler … (7.61)
> To accept it without arrogance, to let it go with indifference. (8.33)

The philosophical tradition may have been influential on another element that we find occasionally: the intermittent snatches of dialogue or quasi-dialogue. As a developed form, the philosophical dialogue goes back to Plato, who was imitated by later philosophers, notably Aristotle (in his lost works) and Cicero. The *Meditations* certainly does not contain the kind of elaborate scene setting that we expect in a true dialogue, but we do find in a number of entries a kind of internal debate in which the questions or objections of an imaginary interlocutor are answered by a second, calmer voice which corrects or rebukes its errors. The first voice seems to represent Marcus's weaker, human side; the second is the voice of philosophy.

The longer entries (none, of course, are very long) are marked by a coherent if sometimes slightly labored style. Not all critics have had kind words for Marcus's expository prose, and some have been inclined to attribute perceived shortcomings to deficiencies in his Greek. But in all likelihood the occasional awkwardness is due less to an imperfect grasp of the language than to roughness of composition—Marcus thinking aloud or groping for an idea. The same explanation may underlie one of the most noticeable features of Marcus's prose—namely, his tendency to string together pairs of near-synonymous words and phrases, as if uncertain whether he has hit the target the first time. When combined with the very abstract vocabulary natural in philosophical prose, this can make for difficult reading, especially in English, which privileges concision and concrete vocabulary to a greater degree than Greek. At its best, however, Marcus's writing can be extraordinarily effective, most of all when it strikes a balance between image and idea, as in the opening of 5.23:

> Keep in mind how fast things pass by and are gone—those that are now, and those to come. Existence flows past us like a river: the "what" is in constant flux, the "why" has a thousand variations. Nothing is stable, not even what's right here. The infinity of past and future gapes before us—a chasm whose depths we cannot see.

This particular topic—the transience of human life, the constant change that shapes and informs the world—is a recurrent theme in the *Meditations,* and as we shall see, it is one whose treatment owes as much to literary as to philosophical models, and as much to Marcus's own character as to Stoic doctrine.

RECURRING THEMES

To try to extract a sustained and coherent argument from the *Meditations* as a whole would be an unprofitable exercise. It is simply not that kind of work. It would be equally fruitless to try to read autobiographical elements into individual entries (to take 9.42 as referring to the revolt of Avidius Cassius, for example, or 10.4 as a reflection on Commodus)—all the more so since so few of the entries can be dated with any security. This is not to say that the *Meditations* has no unity or no relationship to Marcus's own life, for it has both. What unifies it is the recurrence of a small number of themes that surely reflect Marcus's own preoccupations. It is the points to which Marcus returns most often that offer the best insight into his character and concerns.

One example that will strike almost any reader is the sense of mortality that pervades the work. Death is not to be feared, Marcus continually reminds himself. It is a natural process, part of the continual change that forms the world. At other points it is the ultimate consolation. "Soon you will be dead," Marcus tells himself on a number of occasions, "and none of it will matter" (cf. 4.6, 7.22, 8.2). The emphasis on the vanity and worthlessness of earthly concerns is here linked to the more general idea of transience. All things change or pass away, perish and are forgotten. This is the burden of several of the thought exercises that Marcus sets himself: to think of the court of Augustus (8.31), of the age of Vespasian or Trajan (4.32), the great philosophers and thinkers of the past (6.47)—all now dust and ashes.

This theme is not specific to Stoicism. We meet it at every turn in ancient literature. Marcus himself quotes the famous passage in Book 6 of Homer's *Iliad* in which the lives of mortals are compared to leaves that grow in the spring, flourish for a season and then fall and die, to be replaced by others (10.34). He would have recognized the sentiment in other writers too, from the melancholy Greek lyric poet Mimnermus, who develops and expands on Homer's simile, to the Roman lawyer Servius Sulpicius, writing to his friend Cicero on the death of the latter's daughter:

> I want to share with you something that brought me not a little consolation, in hopes that it might have the same effect on you. On my way back from Asia, on the voyage from Aegina to Megara, I gazed at the lands we passed. Aegina was behind me, Megara before me, Piraeus on the starboard side, Corinth to port—towns which flourished once upon a time, and now lie fallen and in ruins before our eyes—and I said to myself, "Alas!...and will you, Servius, not restrain your grief and recall that you were born a mortal?" Believe me, the thought was no small consolation to me.

This is not a point modern grief counselors would be inclined to dwell on, but it is one that Marcus would have understood perfectly, and its appeal to him casts light on both his character and his background. Marcus may have been a Stoic, but he was also a Roman, influenced not only by Zeno and Chrysippus but by Homer and Vergil. Vergil is nowhere mentioned in the *Meditations,* and in a Greek work could hardly be quoted or alluded to, but there is a note of melancholy that runs through the work that one can only call Vergilian.

Other concerns surface as well. A number of entries discuss methods of dealing with pain or bodily weakness of other sorts. "When you have trouble getting out of bed..." begin several entries (5.1, 8.12). A persistent motif is the need to restrain anger and irritation with other people, to put up with their incompetence or malice, to show them the errors of their ways. Several entries focus on the frustrations of life at court, nowhere more present than when Marcus tells himself to stop complaining about them (8.9). He contrasts the court against philosophy as a stepmother against a mother—to be visited out of duty, but not someone we can really love (6.12). Yet the court need not be an obstacle: it can be a challenge, even an opportunity. One can lead a good life anywhere, even at court, as Antoninus showed (5.16, 1.16). "No role [is] so well suited to philosophy," Marcus tells himself, "as the one you happen to be in right now" (11.7).

A more subtle clue to Marcus's personality is the imagery that he prefers. It is worth noting, for example, how many images of nature occur in the *Meditations*. Many readers have been struck by *Meditations* 3.2, with its evocation of "nature's inadvertence" in baking bread or ripening figs, olives, and stalks of wheat. Metaphors and offhand comparisons in other entries evoke the pastoral and agricultural rhythms of the Mediterranean world, with its flocks, herds, and vines, its seasons of sowing and harvesting, its grapes drying slowly into raisins. Some of these may be stock examples, but even a stock example can be revealing. One can hardly read a page of Plato without tripping over the helmsmen, doctors, shoemakers, and other craftsmen who populated ancient Athens; such figures are much rarer in Marcus. The image of society as a tree whose branches are individual human beings expresses an important Stoic principle, but the image is developed further than one might expect and informed by what might be personal observation: "You can see the difference between the branch that's been there since the beginning, remaining on the tree and growing with it, and the one that's been cut off and grafted back."

Affection for the natural world contrasts with a persistent sense of disgust and contempt for human life and other human beings—a sense that it is difficult to derive from (or even reconcile with) Stoicism. As P. A. Brunt puts it, "Reason told Marcus that the world was good beyond improvement, and yet it constantly appeared to him evil beyond remedy." The courtiers who surround him are vain and obsequious, while the people he deals with on a daily basis are "meddling, ungrateful, arrogant, dishonest, jealous, and surly" (2.1). One of the most frequently recurring points in the *Meditations* is the reminder that human beings are social animals, as if this was a point Marcus had a particularly hard time accepting. The gods care for mortals, he reminds himself, "and you—on the verge of death— you still refuse to care for them."

There is a persistent strain of pessimism in the work. "The things we want in life are empty, stale, and trivial. Dogs snarling at each other. Quarreling children—laughing and then bursting into tears a moment later. Trust, shame, justice, truth—'gone from the earth and only found in heaven.' Why are you still here?" (5.33). Images of dirt appear in several entries. The world around us resembles the baths: "oil, sweat, dirt, grayish water, all of it disgust- ing" (8.24). If Marcus contemplates the stars, he does so only in order to "wash off the mud of life below" (7.47). And the objective analysis Marcus prizes often shades over into a depressing cynicism (in the modern sense of the term). "Disgust at what things are made of: Liquid, dust, bones, filth. Or marble as hardened dirt, gold and silver as residues, clothes as hair, purple dye as shellfish blood. And all the rest" (9.36). The human body itself is no more than "rotting meat in a bag" (8.38). "[D]espise your flesh. A mess of blood, pieces of bone, a woven tangle of nerves, veins, arteries" (2.2). Perhaps the most depressing entry in the entire work is the one in which Mar- cus urges himself to cultivate an indifference to music (11.2).

As one scholar has observed, "reading the *Meditations* for long periods can be conducive of melancholy." And even those who love the book cannot deny that there is something impoverishing about the view of human life it presents. Matthew Arnold, whose essay on the work reveals a deep respect and affection for Marcus, identified the central shortcoming of his philosophy as its failure to make any allowance for joy, and I think this is a fair criticism. Marcus does not offer us a means of achieving happiness, but only a means of resisting pain. The Stoicism of the *Meditations* is fundamentally a defensive philosophy; it is noteworthy how many military images recur, from references to the soul as being "posted" or "stationed" to the famous image of the mind as an invulnerable fortress (8.48). Such images are not unique to Marcus, but one can imagine that they might have had special meaning for an emperor whose last years were spent in "*warfare and a journey far from home*" (2.17). For Marcus, life was a battle, and often it must have seemed—what in some sense it must always be—a losing battle.

There are also a handful of points in the text where we have glimpses of a different frame of mind, most obviously when Marcus refers to the gods. From a Stoic perspective, of course, "God" or "the gods" (the terms are used interchangeably by many ancient writers) are merely conventional terms for what we might equally well call "nature" or "the *logos*" or "Providence," or simply "how things are." Marcus stresses the benevolence of this power (what is divine must be good, surely?), but it is clear that he also ascribes to its actions the implacability with which orthodox Stoic doctrine endows it. It is not easy to see why one should pray to a power whose decisions one can hardly hope to influence, and indeed Marcus several times seems to admit the possibility that one should not (5.7, 6.44, 9.40).

It is all the more surprising, then, to find Marcus elsewhere suggesting a more personal concern on the gods' part. The final entry of Book 1 is the most obvious example. Here Marcus indicates that the gods have aided him quite directly "through their gifts, their help, their inspiration," just as they have others (cf. 9.11). Their help is curiously concrete. Among the things for which they are thanked are "remedies granted through dreams," including "the one at Caieta" (1.17; the text is uncertain). The gods also assist other people, he reminds himself, "just as they do you—by signs and dreams and every other way" (9.27). That Marcus himself did believe deeply in the gods, not merely as a figure of speech but as a real force in his own life, is suggested by his refutation of those who doubt their existence: "I know the gods exist....—from having felt their power, over and over" (12.28). How was this personal relationship with the divine to be reconciled with the impersonal *logos* of the Stoics? The question seems to be played out in the dialogue at *Meditations* 9.40. "But those are things the gods left up to me," protests one voice, to which another responds, "And what makes you think the gods don't care about what's up to us?" Marcus himself may not have fully recognized or acknowledged this conflict, but its existence may point to a half-conscious awareness that the answer Stoicism offered was not in every respect satisfactory.

LATER INFLUENCE

How or by whom the *Meditations* was preserved is unknown. The late-fourth-century *Historia Augusta* paints a picture of Marcus lecturing on the *Meditations* to a spellbound audience at Rome—one of the charming fantasies in which that peculiar work abounds, but certainly an invention. The passage does suggest, however, that the text was in circulation by the fourth century, when it is also mentioned by the orator Themistius. It was very likely familiar also to a contemporary of Themistius's, the neo-pagan emperor Julian (known to later ages as Julian the Apostate), in whose dialogue "The Caesars" Marcus is pictured as a model for the kind of philosopher-king that Julian himself aspired to be.

The century that followed Themistius and Julian was one of decline, at least in the West—decline in political institutions, and also in the knowledge of Greek. For the next thousand years Marcus's work, like that of Homer and Euripides, would remain unknown to Western readers. Copies survived in the Greek-speaking East, of course, but even there the *Meditations* seems to have been little read. For centuries, all trace of it is lost, until at the beginning of the tenth century it reappears in a letter from the scholar and churchman Arethas, who writes to a friend, "I have had for a while now a copy of the Emperor Marcus's invaluable book. It was not only old but practically coming apart....I have had it copied and can now pass it on to posterity in better shape." Whether Arethas's copy was indeed responsible for the work's survival we do not know. At any rate, its readership seems to have increased in the centuries that followed. It is quoted a generation or two later by the vast Byzantine encyclopedia known as the *Suda*, and it was perhaps around this period also that an unknown Byzantine poet composed a brief appreciation that came to be copied along with the text:

ON THE BOOK OF MARCUS

If you desire to master pain
Unroll this book and read with care,
And in it find abundantly
A knowledge of the things that are,
Those that have been, and those to come.

And know as well that joy and grief
Are nothing more than empty smoke.

The fall of Constantinople to the Turks in 1453 led to an exodus of scholars, bringing with them the Greek texts that inspired the Italian Renaissance. The *Meditations* must have been among them. Yet even at this date the work's survival hung by a thread. The only complete manuscript to survive is a fourteenth-century codex (now in the Vatican), which is riddled with errors. The first printed edition did not appear until 1559, when Wilhelm Holzmann (known as Xylander) produced a text from what seems to have been a more reliable manuscript. That manuscript, unfortunately, has not survived. But even at its best it was a very imperfect witness to what Marcus himself wrote. Our text of the *Meditations* contains a number of passages that are garbled or in which one or more crucial words seem to have been omitted. Some of these errors may be due to the confused state of Marcus's original copy. Others may have been accidentally introduced in the course of the copying and recopying that the work underwent in the millennium following Marcus's death. In some cases the informed guesswork of scholars over several centuries has been able to restore the original text. In others, there is still uncertainty.[11]

The *Meditations* has never attracted great interest from professional students of the classics, and the reasons are perhaps understandable. It contains few direct references to historical events and provides relatively little material for social historians. As evidence for later Stoicism it pales beside the greater bulk of Epictetus's *Discourses*. Yet it has always exerted a fascination on those outside the narrow orbit of classical study, perhaps especially on those who can best appreciate the pressures that Marcus himself faced. The *Meditations* was among the favorite reading of Frederick the Great; a recent American president has claimed to reread it every few years. But it has attracted others too, from poets like Pope, Goethe, and Arnold to the southern planter William Alexander Percy, who observed in his autobiography that "there is left to each of us, no matter how far defeat pierces, the unassailable wintry kingdom of

Marcus Aurelius.... It is not outside, but within, and when all is lost, it stands fast."[12]

If Marcus has been studied less than many ancient authors, he has been translated more than most. But it has been a generation since his last English incarnation, and the time seems ripe for another attempt. My intention in what follows has been to represent in readable English both the content and the texture of the *Meditations.* I have been especially concerned to convey the patchwork character of the original, both the epigrammatic concision that characterizes some entries and the straggling discursiveness of others. I hope the results will bear out my conviction that what a Roman emperor wrote long ago for his own use can still be meaningful to those far removed from him in time and space. We do not live in Marcus's world, but it is not as remote from us as we sometimes imagine. There could be no better witness to the effect of the *Meditations* on a modern reader than the Russian poet Joseph Brodsky, whose essay "Homage to Marcus Aurelius" takes its departure from the famous statue of the emperor on the Capitoline hill in Rome:

> I saw him for the last time a few years ago, on a wet winter night, in the company of a stray Dalmatian. I was returning by taxi to my hotel after one of the most disastrous evenings in my entire life. The next morning I was leaving Rome for the States. I was drunk. The traffic moved with the speed one wishes for one's funeral. At the foot of the Capitol I asked the driver to stop, paid, and got out of the car.... Presently I discovered I was not alone: a middle-sized Dalmatian appeared out of nowhere and quietly sat down a couple of feet away. Its sudden presence was so oddly comforting that momentarily I felt like offering it one of my cigarettes.... For a while we both stared at the horseman's statue.... And suddenly—presumably because of the rain and the rhythmic pattern of Michelangelo's pilasters and arches—all got blurred,

and against that blur, the shining statue, devoid of any geometry, seemed to be moving. Not at great speed, and not out of this place; but enough for the Dalmatian to leave my side and follow the bronze progress.

FURTHER READING

The standard modern biography of Marcus is A. R. Birley, *Marcus Aurelius* (1966; rev. ed., New Haven, Conn.: Yale University Press, 1987), which makes full use of the principal ancient literary sources—not only the *Meditations* (especially Book 1), but the remains of the history of Dio Cassius, the letters of Fronto and the biography of Marcus in the so-called *Historia Augusta*. Birley also draws on recent research into the careers of upper-class officc-holders (prosopography) and the workings of the imperial admin-istration to paint a picture of Marcus's background and the society he moved in.

The most comprehensive and reliable treatment of the Anto-nine age can be found in the *Cambridge Ancient History*, volume XI, *The High Empire, A.D. 70–192* (Cambridge University Press, 2000). Edward Gibbon's famous characterization of the period in the opening chapters of his *History of the Decline and Fall of the Roman Empire* remains well worth reading, although the picture it paints may be too rosy-colored. A useful counterbalance is E. R. Dodds, *Pagan and Christian in an Age of Anxiety* (Cambridge, Eng.: Cam-bridge University Press, 1965), which offers a very different assess-ment of the period.

Treatments of special topics abound, and only a few titles can be mentioned. The upper-class education that Marcus enjoyed is described by S. F. Bonner, *Education in Ancient Rome* (Berkeley: Uni-versity of California Press, 1977). E. Champlin's *Fronto and Anto-*

nine Rome (Cambridge, Mass.: Harvard University Press, 1980) is the best modern study of Marcus's teacher. Glen Bowersock's *Greek Sophists in the Roman Empire* (Oxford: Oxford University Press, 1969) is a fundamental study of intellectual culture in the second century. Fergus Millar's *The Emperor in the Roman World* (Ithaca, N.Y.: Cornell University Press, 1977) is an exhaustive analysis of the civil and administrative functions performed by Marcus and his fellow emperors, complemented for military matters by J. B. Campbell's *The Emperor and the Roman Army* (Oxford: Oxford University Press, 1984).

Most of the major ancient sources for Marcus and his world are conveniently printed with facing-page English translations in the Loeb Classical Library. The valuable but highly unreliable life of Marcus in the *Historia Augusta* can be found in the three volumes of *Scriptores Historiae Augustae,* trans. D. Magie (1921–1932), as well as in A. Birley, trans., *Lives of the Later Caesars* (New York: Penguin, 1976). The Loeb series also includes the letters of Fronto, trans. C. R. Haines (2 volumes, 1919); and of the historian Dio Cassius, trans. E. Cary (9 volumes, 1914–1927, of which the last two are relevant to Marcus). Although composed and collected a generation before Marcus's birth, the *Letters of Pliny the Younger,* trans. Betty Radice (2 volumes, 1969), are a rich and illuminating source for upper-class society in the mid-empire. Insight into the intellectual life of the period can be gained from the *Attic Nights* of the antiquarian Aulus Gellius, trans. J. C. Rolfe (3 volumes, 1927), the works of the satirist Lucian, trans. A. M. Harmon, K. Kilburn and M. D. MacLeod (8 volumes, 1913–1967), and Philostratus's entertaining *Lives of the Sophists,* trans. W. C. Wright (1921). Finally, mention should be made of two modern novels set in the Antonine period, Walter Pater's *Marius the Epicurean* (1885) and Marguerite Yourcenar's *Memoirs of Hadrian* (1951). Neither should be mistaken for a primary source, but each is, in its different way, a masterpiece.

Recent work on Hellenistic philosophy has done much to illuminate the philosophical background of the *Meditations*. A clear and helpful introduction to both Stoicism and Epicureanism can be found in A. A. Long, *Hellenistic Philosophy* (London: Duckworth, 1974); on a much larger scale is Keimpe Algra, Jonathan Barnes and Jaap Mansfeld, eds., *The Cambridge History of Hellenistic Philosophy* (New York: Cambridge University Press, 1999). On Stoicism see also F. H. Sandbach, *The Stoics* (London: Chatto and Windus, 1975), and J. Rist, *Stoic Philosophy* (Cambridge, Eng.: Cambridge University Press, 1969). The works of the two most important Stoics, Zeno and Chrysippus, are largely lost; their surviving fragments are translated in the first volume of A. A. Long and David Sedley, *The Hellenistic Philosophers* (New York: Cambridge University Press, 1987), which also includes much material on Epicureanism. An important source for the history of both schools is Diogenes Laertius's *Lives of the Philosophers*, trans. R. D. Hicks, in the Loeb series (2 volumes, 1925).[13]

For Stoicism under the empire, the most important sources are the works of Seneca the Younger and Epictetus. The best introduction to Seneca is probably the *Letters to Lucilius*, of which a selection is available in *Letters from a Stoic*, trans. R. Campbell (New York: Penguin, 1969). Epictetus's *Discourses* and the *Encheiridion* are available in the Loeb series in a translation by W. A. Oldfather (2 volumes, 1925). The *Encheiridion* has also been translated by T. W. Higginson (Indianapolis: Bobbs-Merrill, 1955).

For the *Meditations* itself the indispensable resource (though long out of print and difficult to obtain) is A.S.L. Farquharson's *The Meditations of the Emperor Marcus Antoninus*, 2 vols. (Oxford, Eng.: Oxford University Press, 1944). I have derived benefit from a number of earlier English translations, notably those of Farquharson (recently reprinted with a new introduction by R. B. Rutherford); George Long (1862); C. R. Haines (Loeb, 1916); G.M.A. Grube (Indianapolis: Bobbs-Merrill, 1963) and Maxwell Staniforth (New York: Penguin, 1964), as well as from W. Theiler's German translation (Zurich: Artemis, 1951) and the French edition of Book 1 by Pierre Hadot (Paris: Les Belles Lettres, 1998). The best modern edition of the Greek text is that by J. Dalfen (2d ed., B. G. Teubner, 1987), though in vexed passages I have sometimes preferred different readings.

Among scholarly studies of the *Meditations,* three in particular deserve mention. P. A. Brunt, "Marcus Aurelius in His *Meditations,*" *Journal of Roman Studies* 64 (1974): 1–20, analyzes the themes that especially exercise Marcus. Pierre Hadot, *The Inner Citadel: The "Meditations" of Marcus Aurelius,* trans. M. Chase (Cambridge, Mass.: Harvard University Press, 1998), is a thoughtful reconstruction of Marcus's philosophical system. R. B. Rutherford, *The Meditations of Marcus Aurelius: A Study* (Oxford, Eng.: Clarendon, 1989), is an excellent analysis from a more literary perspective, with good remarks also on Marcus's relationship with the gods. Among the many appreciations by nonclassicists two deserve special mention: Matthew Arnold's "Marcus Aurelius" (originally a review of Long's translation) in his *Lectures and Essays in Criticism,* ed. R. H. Super (Ann Arbor: University of Michigan Press, 1962), and Joseph Brodsky's "Homage to Marcus Aurelius" in his collection *On Grief and Reason* (New York: Farrar, Straus and Giroux, 1995).

ACKNOWLEDGMENTS

Karen Schwabach read through an initial draft of the translation and suggested numerous improvements, for which I am deeply grateful.

For help of various sorts I am also indebted to Deborah DeMania, Gregory Gelburd, Krista Kane, Charles Mathewes, Katherine Odell, Hayden Pelliccia, Ellyn Schumacher, and Alphonse Vinh. My colleagues in the Department of Classics at the University of Virginia, and in particular my department chair, John Miller, made it possible for me to take course relief during the fall semester of 2001, when much of the work was completed. Thanks are due finally to my editor, Will Murphy, for his patience and enthusiasm for this project.

INTRODUCTION NOTES

1. In this larger sense, rather than attempting to translate it, I have generally left it simply as "(the) *logos.*" I hope that readers who have assimilated such terms as "karma" and "the Tao" will be prepared to welcome this one too.
2. So, too, some modern physicists have imagined a series of universes produced by an alternation of expansions and contractions—"big bangs" and "big crunches."
3. Ramsay Macmullen, *Enemies of the Roman Order* (Cambridge, Mass.: Harvard University Press, 1966), p. 48.
4. Earlier translators have been driven to clumsy equivalents such as "Guiding Reason." I have generally rendered it "mind," as being perhaps the least unsatisfactory English equivalent.
5. Two examples are worth pointing to. Marcus finds the gladiatorial combat and the brutal executions of the arena a source of tedium (6.46); that they might be morally wrong seems never to have occurred to him. He prides himself on not having taken sexual advantage of his slaves, not because it would have been harmful or unjust to them, but because such self-indulgence would have been damaging to his own character (1.17). There is no sign that he ever questioned slavery as an institution. If asked, he would no doubt have responded that "true" slavery is the self-enslavement of the mind to emotion and desire (cf. 8.3, 9.40, 11.30); actual bodily slavery is merely a condition to be accepted and endured, like nearsightedness or a cold.

6. A still better title might be "Memoranda," which suggests both the miscellaneous character of the work and something about its intended function. Scores of entries begin with the injunctions to "remember..." or "keep in mind...," while the syntax of others (e.g., 12.18) presupposes such an admonition.

7. In order to stress the self-directed nature of the *Meditations* I have sometimes preferred to translate these as resolutions ("to...") rather than direct commands.

8. The conventional divisions and numbering go back only to the Latin translation published by Thomas Gataker in 1652. It cannot be regarded as authoritative, and I have occasionally split up a single entry into two (sometimes following earlier editors, sometimes not).

9. There are some striking omissions, which may or may not be significant. Antoninus's predecessor, Hadrian, is not mentioned, for example. It may be that Marcus disapproved of him, or simply that he had little contact with him before his death in 138. Perhaps more surprising is the lack of any reference to Herodes Atticus, from whom Marcus learned Greek rhetoric. Does this point to personal tensions that arose between the two in later years? Or does the omission stem from Marcus's move away from rhetoric toward philosophy? (It is noteworthy that the Latin rhetorician Fronto, with whom Marcus seems to have been close, is allotted only a very brief entry in comparison with Marcus's philosophical preceptors.)

10. The openings of Books 2 and 3 differ from those that follow in including a brief note to identify (presumably) the place of composition. We do not know whether these notes go back to Marcus himself, or why the other books lack them. The average length of the entries in these two books is perhaps slightly longer than in the later books, but there are few differences otherwise. Attempts to find a thematic thread within Books 2 and 3 as a whole are not convincing.

11. I have noted the most egregious instances in the notes, and have marked with an obelus (< ... >) a few passages where the original is impossible to reconstruct.

12. William Alexander Percy, *Lanterns on the Levee* (Baton Rouge: Louisiana State University Press, 1973), p. 313.

13. A survey of work on the predecessors and rivals of the Stoics is obviously beyond the scope of this note, but two good starting points may be mentioned. The surviving fragments of Heraclitus and other early philosophers who appear in the *Meditations* are translated in Kathleen

Freeman, *Ancilla to the Presocratic Philosophers* (Oxford: Blackwell, 1948 and later reprints). Any reader unfamiliar with Plato should probably begin with the *Apology of Socrates,* available in the Modern Library's *Selected Dialogues of Plato,* trans. B. Jowett, rev. H. Pelliccia (New York: Random House, 2000) or any number of other translations.

CHRONOLOGY

	HISTORICAL	LITERARY/PHILOSOPHICAL
500		Heraclitus
		Empedocles
		Democritus
400		Socrates
		Plato
		Diogenes
300	Alexander the Great	Zeno, Epicurus
		Chrysippus
200		
100		
	Pompey, Caesar	
	Augustus	
B.C./A.D.	Tiberius	
	Nero	Thrasea Paetus
	Vespasian	Helvidius Priscus
	Domitian	Epictetus
100	Trajan	
	Hadrian	
	Antoninus Pius	Fronto
	Marcus Aurelius	
200		

MEDITATIONS

BOOK 1

DEBTS AND LESSONS

1. MY GRANDFATHER VERUS

Character and self-control.

2. MY FATHER (FROM MY OWN MEMORIES AND HIS REPUTATION)

Integrity and manliness.

3. MY MOTHER

Her reverence for the divine, her generosity, her inability not only to do wrong but even to conceive of doing it. And the simple way she lived—not in the least like the rich.

4. MY GREAT-GRANDFATHER

To avoid the public schools, to hire good private teachers, and to accept the resulting costs as money well-spent.

5. MY FIRST TEACHER

Not to support this side or that in chariot-racing, this fighter or that in the games. To put up with discomfort and not make demands. To do my own work, mind my own business, and have no time for slanderers.

6. DIOGNETUS

Not to waste time on nonsense. Not to be taken in by conjurors and hoodoo artists with their talk about incantations and exorcism and all the rest of it. Not to be obsessed with quail-fighting or other crazes like that. To hear unwelcome truths. To practice philosophy, and to study with Baccheius, and then with Tandasis and Marcianus. To write dialogues as a student. To choose the Greek lifestyle—the camp-bed and the cloak.

7. RUSTICUS

The recognition that I needed to train and discipline my character.

Not to be sidetracked by my interest in rhetoric. Not to write treatises on abstract questions, or deliver moralizing little sermons, or compose imaginary descriptions of The Simple Life or The Man Who Lives Only for Others. To steer clear of oratory, poetry and *belles lettres.*

Not to dress up just to stroll around the house, or things like that. To write straightforward letters (like the one he sent my mother from Sinuessa). And to behave in a conciliatory way when people who have angered or annoyed us want to make up.

To read attentively—not to be satisfied with "just getting the gist of it." And not to fall for every smooth talker.

And for introducing me to Epictetus's lectures—and loaning me his own copy.

8. APOLLONIUS

Independence and unvarying reliability, and to pay attention to nothing, no matter how fleetingly, except the *logos.* And to be the same in all circumstances—intense pain, the loss of a child, chronic illness. And to see clearly, from his example, that a man can show both strength and flexibility.

His patience in teaching. And to have seen someone who clearly viewed his expertise and ability as a teacher as the humblest of virtues.

And to have learned how to accept favors from friends without losing your self-respect or appearing ungrateful.

9. SEXTUS

Kindness.

An example of fatherly authority in the home. What it means to live as nature requires.

Gravity without airs.

To show intuitive sympathy for friends, tolerance to amateurs and sloppy thinkers. His ability to get along with everyone: sharing his company was the highest of compliments, and the opportunity an honor for those around him.

To investigate and analyze, with understanding and logic, the principles we ought to live by.

Not to display anger or other emotions. To be free of passion and yet full of love.

To praise without bombast; to display expertise without pretension.

10. THE LITERARY CRITIC ALEXANDER

Not to be constantly correcting people, and in particular not to jump on them whenever they make an error of usage or a grammatical mistake or mispronounce something, but just answer their question or add another example, or debate the issue itself (not their phrasing), or make some other contribution to the discussion—and insert the right expression, unobtrusively.

11. FRONTO

To recognize the malice, cunning, and hypocrisy that power produces, and the peculiar ruthlessness often shown by people from "good families."

12. ALEXANDER THE PLATONIST

Not to be constantly telling people (or writing them) that I'm too busy, unless I really am. Similarly, not to be always ducking my responsibilities to the people around me because of "pressing business."

13. CATULUS

Not to shrug off a friend's resentment—even unjustified resentment—but try to put things right.

To show your teachers ungrudging respect (the Domitius and Athenodotus story), and your children unfeigned love.

14. [MY BROTHER] SEVERUS

To love my family, truth and justice. It was through him that I encountered Thrasea, Helvidius, Cato, Dion and Brutus, and conceived of a society of equal laws, governed by equality of status and of speech, and of rulers who respect the liberty of their subjects above all else.

And from him as well, to be steady and consistent in valuing philosophy.

And to help others and be eager to share, not to be a pessimist, and never to doubt your friends' affection for you. And that when people incurred his disapproval, they always knew it. And that his friends never had to speculate about his attitude to anything: it was always clear.

15. MAXIMUS

Self-control and resistance to distractions.
Optimism in adversity—especially illness.

A personality in balance: dignity and grace together.

Doing your job without whining.

Other people's certainty that what he said was what he
     thought, and what he did was done without malice.

Never taken aback or apprehensive. Neither rash nor
     hesitant—or bewildered, or at a loss. Not obsequious—but
     not aggressive or paranoid either.

Generosity, charity, honesty.

The sense he gave of *staying* on the path rather than being *kept*
     on it.

That no one could ever have felt patronized by him—or in a
     position to patronize him.

A sense of humor.

16. MY ADOPTED FATHER

Compassion. Unwavering adherence to decisions, once he'd
reached them. Indifference to superficial honors. Hard work. Per-
sistence.

Listening to anyone who could contribute to the public good.

His dogged determination to treat people as they deserved.

A sense of when to push and when to back off.

Putting a stop to the pursuit of boys.

His altruism. Not expecting his friends to keep him entertained
at dinner or to travel with him (unless they wanted to). And anyone
who had to stay behind to take care of something always found him
the same when he returned.

His searching questions at meetings. A kind of single-
mindedness, almost, never content with first impressions, or breaking off the discussion prematurely.

His constancy to friends—never getting fed up with them, or
playing favorites.

Self-reliance, always. And cheerfulness.

And his advance planning (well in advance) and his discreet attention to even minor things.

His restrictions on acclamations—and all attempts to flatter him.

His constant devotion to the empire's needs. His stewardship of the treasury. His willingness to take responsibility—and blame—for both.

His attitude to the gods: no superstitiousness. And his attitude to men: no demagoguery, no currying favor, no pandering. Always sober, always steady, and never vulgar or a prey to fads.

The way he handled the material comforts that fortune had supplied him in such abundance—without arrogance and without apology. If they were there, he took advantage of them. If not, he didn't miss them.

No one ever called him glib, or shameless, or pedantic. They saw him for what he was: a man tested by life, accomplished, unswayed by flattery, qualified to govern both himself and them.

His respect for people who practiced philosophy—at least, those who were sincere about it. But without denigrating the others—or listening to them.

His ability to feel at ease with people—and put them at *their* ease, without being pushy.

His willingness to take adequate care of himself. Not a hypochondriac or obsessed with his appearance, but not ignoring things either. With the result that he hardly ever needed medical attention, or drugs or any sort of salve or ointment.

This, in particular: his willingness to yield the floor to experts—in oratory, law, psychology, whatever—and to support them energetically, so that each of them could fulfill his potential.

That he respected tradition without needing to constantly congratulate himself for Safeguarding Our Traditional Values.

Not prone to go off on tangents, or pulled in all directions, but sticking with the same old places and the same old things.

The way he could have one of his migraines and then go right back to what he was doing—fresh and at the top of his game.

That he had so few secrets—only state secrets, in fact, and not all that many of those.

The way he kept public actions within reasonable bounds— games, building projects, distributions of money and so on— because he looked to what needed doing and not the credit to be gained from doing it.

No bathing at strange hours, no self-indulgent building projects, no concern for food, or the cut and color of his clothes, or having attractive slaves. (The robe from his farm at Lorium, most of the things at Lanuvium, the way he accepted the customs agent's apology at Tusculum, etc.)

He never exhibited rudeness, lost control of himself, or turned violent. No one ever saw him sweat. Everything was to be approached logically and with due consideration, in a calm and orderly fashion but decisively, and with no loose ends.

You could have said of him (as they say of Socrates) that he knew how to enjoy and abstain from things that most people find it hard to abstain from and all too easy to enjoy. Strength, perseverance, self-control in both areas: the mark of a soul in readiness— indomitable.

(Maximus's illness.)

17. THE GODS

That I had good grandparents, a good mother and father, a good sister, good teachers, good servants, relatives, friends—almost without exception. And that I never lost control of myself with any of them, although I had it in me to do that, and I might have, easily. But thanks to the gods, I was never put in that position, and so escaped the test.

That I wasn't raised by my grandfather's girlfriend for longer than I was. That I didn't lose my virginity too early, and didn't enter adulthood until it was time—put it off, even.

That I had someone—as a ruler and as a father—who could keep me from being arrogant and make me realize that even at court you can live without a troop of bodyguards, and gorgeous clothes, lamps, sculpture—the whole charade. That you can behave almost like an ordinary person without seeming slovenly or careless as a ruler or when carrying out official obligations.

That I had the kind of brother I did. One whose character challenged me to improve my own. One whose love and affection enriched my life.

That my children weren't born stupid or physically deformed.

That I wasn't more talented in rhetoric or poetry, or other areas. If I'd felt that I was making better progress I might never have given them up.

That I conferred on the people who brought me up the honors they seemed to want early on, instead of putting them off (since they were still young) with the hope that I'd do it later.

That I knew Apollonius, and Rusticus, and Maximus.

That I was shown clearly and often what it would be like to live as nature requires. The gods did all they could—through their gifts, their help, their inspiration—to ensure that I could live as nature demands. And if I've failed, it's no one's fault but mine. Because I didn't pay attention to what they told me—to what they taught me, practically, step by step.

That my body has held out, especially considering the life I've led.

That I never laid a finger on Benedicta or on Theodotus. And that even later, when I was overcome by passion, I recovered from it.

That even though I was often upset with Rusticus I never did anything I would have regretted later.

That even though she died young, at least my mother spent her last years with me.

That whenever I felt like helping someone who was short of money, or otherwise in need, I never had to be told that I had no resources to do it with. And that I was never put in that position myself—of having to take something from someone else.

That I have the wife I do: obedient, loving, humble.

That my children had competent teachers.

Remedies granted through dreams—when I was coughing blood, for instance, and having fits of dizziness. And the one at Caieta.

That when I became interested in philosophy I didn't fall into the hands of charlatans, and didn't get bogged down in writing treatises, or become absorbed by logic-chopping, or preoccupied with physics.

All things for which "we need the help of fortune and the gods."

BOOK 2

ON THE RIVER GRAN,
AMONG THE QUADI

1. When you wake up in the morning, tell yourself: The people I deal with today will be meddling, ungrateful, arrogant, dishonest, jealous, and surly. They are like this because they can't tell good from evil. But I have seen the beauty of good, and the ugliness of evil, and have recognized that the wrongdoer has a nature related to my own—not of the same blood or birth, but the same mind, and possessing a share of the divine. And so none of them can hurt me. No one can implicate me in ugliness. Nor can I feel angry at my relative, or hate him. We were born to work together like feet, hands, and eyes, like the two rows of teeth, upper and lower. To obstruct each other is unnatural. To feel anger at someone, to turn your back on him: these are obstructions.

2. Whatever this is that I am, it is flesh and a little spirit and an intelligence. Throw away your books; stop letting yourself be distracted. That is not allowed. Instead, as if you were dying right now, despise your flesh. A mess of blood, pieces of bone, a woven tangle of nerves, veins, arteries. Consider what the spirit is: air, and never the same air, but vomited out and gulped in again every instant. Finally, the intelligence. Think of it this way: You are an old man. Stop allowing your mind to be a slave, to be jerked about by selfish impulses, to kick against fate and the present, and to mistrust the future.

3. What is divine is full of Providence. Even chance is not divorced from nature, from the inweaving and enfolding of things governed by Providence. Everything proceeds from it. And then there is necessity and the needs of the whole world, of which you are a part. Whatever the nature of the whole does, and whatever serves to maintain it, is good for every part of nature. The world is maintained by change—in the elements and in the things they compose. That should be enough for you; treat it as an axiom. Discard your thirst for books, so that you won't die in bitterness, but in cheerfulness and truth, grateful to the gods from the bottom of your heart.

4. Remember how long you've been putting this off, how many extensions the gods gave you, and you didn't use them. At some point you have to recognize what world it is that you belong to; what power rules it and from what source you spring; that there is a limit to the time assigned you, and if you don't use it to free yourself it will be gone and will never return.

5. Concentrate every minute like a Roman—like a man—on doing what's in front of you with precise and genuine seriousness, tenderly, willingly, with justice. And on freeing yourself from all other distractions. Yes, you can—if you do everything as if it were the last thing you were doing in your life, and stop being aimless, stop letting your emotions override what your mind tells you, stop being hypocritical, self-centered, irritable. You see how few things you have to do to live a satisfying and reverent life? If you can manage this, that's all even the gods can ask of you.

6. Yes, keep on degrading yourself, soul. But soon your chance at dignity will be gone. Everyone gets one life. Yours is almost used up,

and instead of treating yourself with respect, you have entrusted your own happiness to the souls of others.

7. Do external things distract you? Then make time for yourself to learn something worthwhile; stop letting yourself be pulled in all directions. But make sure you guard against the other kind of confusion. People who labor all their lives but have no purpose to direct every thought and impulse toward are wasting their time—even when hard at work.

8. Ignoring what goes on in other people's souls—no one ever came to grief that way. But if you won't keep track of what your *own* soul's doing, how can you *not* be unhappy?

9. Don't ever forget these things:

The nature of the world.
My nature.
How I relate to the world.
What proportion of it I make up.
That you are part of nature, and no one can prevent you
    from speaking and acting in harmony with it, always.

10. In comparing sins (the way people do) Theophrastus says that the ones committed out of desire are worse than the ones committed out of anger: which is good philosophy. The angry man seems to turn his back on reason out of a kind of pain and inner convulsion. But the man motivated by desire, who is mastered by pleasure, seems somehow more self-indulgent, less manly in his sins. Theophrastus is right, and philosophically sound, to say that the sin committed out of pleasure deserves a harsher rebuke than the one committed out of pain. The angry man is more like a victim of

wrongdoing, provoked by pain to anger. The other man rushes into wrongdoing on his own, moved to action by desire.

11. You could leave life right now. Let that determine what you do and say and think. If the gods exist, then to abandon human beings is not frightening; the gods would never subject you to harm. And if they don't exist, or don't care what happens to us, what would be the point of living in a world without gods or Providence? But they do exist, they do care what happens to us, and everything a person needs to avoid real harm they have placed within him. If there were anything harmful on the other side of death, they would have made sure that the ability to avoid it was within you. If it doesn't harm your character, how can it harm your life? Nature would not have overlooked such dangers through failing to recognize them, or because it saw them but was powerless to prevent or correct them. Nor would it ever, through inability or incompetence, make such a mistake as to let good and bad things happen indiscriminately to good and bad alike. But death and life, success and failure, pain and pleasure, wealth and poverty, all these happen to good and bad alike, and they are neither noble nor shameful—and hence neither good nor bad.

12. The speed with which all of them vanish—the objects in the world, and the memory of them in time. And the real nature of the things our senses experience, especially those that entice us with pleasure or frighten us with pain or are loudly trumpeted by pride. To understand those things—how stupid, contemptible, grimy, decaying, and dead they are—that's what our intellectual powers are for. And to understand what those people really amount to, whose opinions and voices constitute fame. And what dying is—and that if you look at it in the abstract and break down your imaginary

ideas of it by logical analysis, you realize that it's nothing but a process of nature, which only children can be afraid of. (And not only a process of nature but a necessary one.) And how man grasps God, with what part of himself he does so, and how that part is conditioned when he does.

13. Nothing is more pathetic than people who run around in circles, "delving into the things that lie beneath" and conducting investigations into the souls of the people around them, never realizing that all you have to do is to be attentive to the power inside you and worship it sincerely. To worship it is to keep it from being muddied with turmoil and becoming aimless and dissatisfied with nature—divine and human. What is divine deserves our respect because it is good; what is human deserves our affection because it is like us. And our pity too, sometimes, for its inability to tell good from bad—as terrible a blindness as the kind that can't tell white from black.

14. Even if you're going to live three thousand more years, or ten times that, remember: you cannot lose another life than the one you're living now, or live another one than the one you're losing. The longest amounts to the same as the shortest. The present is the same for everyone; its loss is the same for everyone; and it should be clear that a brief instant is all that is lost. For you can't lose either the past or the future; how could you lose what you don't have?

Remember two things:

    i. that everything has always been the same, and keeps recurring, and it makes no difference whether you see the same things recur in a hundred years or two hundred, or in an infinite period;

ii. that the longest-lived and those who will die soonest lose the same thing. The present is all that they can give up, since that is all you have, and what you do not have, you cannot lose.

15. "Everything is just an impression." —Monimus the Cynic. And the response is obvious enough. But the point is a useful one, if you take it for what it's worth.

16. The human soul degrades itself:

i. Above all, when it does its best to become an abscess, a kind of detached growth on the world. To be disgruntled at anything that happens is a kind of secession from Nature, which comprises the nature of all things.
ii. When it turns its back on another person or sets out to do it harm, as the souls of the angry do.
iii. When it is overpowered by pleasure or pain.
iv. When it puts on a mask and does or says something artificial or false.
v. When it allows its action and impulse to be without a purpose, to be random and disconnected: even the smallest things ought to be directed toward a goal. But the goal of rational beings is to follow the rule and law of the most ancient of communities and states.

17. Human life.
Duration: *momentary.* Nature: *changeable.* Perception: *dim.* Condition of Body: *decaying.* Soul: *spinning around.* Fortune: *unpredictable.* Lasting Fame: *uncertain.* Sum Up: *The body and its parts are a river, the soul a dream and mist, life is warfare and a journey far from home, lasting reputation is oblivion.*
Then what can guide us?

Only philosophy.

Which means making sure that the power within stays safe and free from assault, superior to pleasure and pain, doing nothing randomly or dishonestly and with imposture, not dependent on anyone else's doing something or not doing it. And making sure that it accepts what happens and what it is dealt as coming from the same place it came from. And above all, that it accepts death in a cheerful spirit, as nothing but the dissolution of the elements from which each living thing is composed. If it doesn't hurt the individual elements to change continually into one another, why are people afraid of all of them changing and separating? It's a natural thing. And nothing natural is evil.

BOOK 3

IN CARNUNTUM

1. Not just that every day more of our life is used up and less and less of it is left, but this too: if we live longer, can we be sure our mind will still be up to understanding the world—to the contemplation that aims at divine and human knowledge? If our mind starts to wander, we'll still go on breathing, go on eating, imagining things, feeling urges and so on. But getting the most out of ourselves, calculating where our duty lies, analyzing what we hear and see, deciding whether it's time to call it quits—all the things you need a healthy mind for . . . all those are gone.

So we need to hurry.

Not just because we move daily closer to death but also because our understanding—our grasp of the world—may be gone before we get there.

2. We should remember that even Nature's inadvertence has its own charm, its own attractiveness. The way loaves of bread split open on top in the oven; the ridges are just by-products of the baking, and yet pleasing, somehow: they rouse our appetite without our knowing why.

Or how ripe figs begin to burst.

And olives on the point of falling: the shadow of decay gives them a peculiar beauty.

Stalks of wheat bending under their own weight. The furrowed brow of the lion. Flecks of foam on the boar's mouth.

And other things. If you look at them in isolation there's nothing beautiful about them, and yet by supplementing nature they enrich it and draw us in. And anyone with a feeling for nature—a deeper sensitivity—will find it all gives pleasure. Even what seems inadvertent. He'll find the jaws of live animals as beautiful as painted ones or sculptures. He'll look calmly at the distinct beauty of old age in men, women, and at the loveliness of children. And other things like that will call out to him constantly—things unnoticed by others. Things seen only by those at home with Nature and its works.

3. Hippocrates cured many illnesses—and then fell ill and died. The Chaldaeans predicted the deaths of many others; in due course their own hour arrived. Alexander, Pompey, Caesar—who utterly destroyed so many cities, cut down so many thousand foot and horse in battle—they too departed this life. Heraclitus often told us the world would end in fire. But it was moisture that carried him off; he died smeared with cowshit. Democritus was killed by ordinary vermin, Socrates by the human kind.

And?

You boarded, you set sail, you've made the passage. Time to disembark. If it's for another life, well, there's nowhere without gods on that side either. If to nothingness, then you no longer have to put up with pain and pleasure, or go on dancing attendance on this battered crate, your body—so much inferior to that which serves it.

One is mind and spirit, the other earth and garbage.

4. Don't waste the rest of your time here worrying about other people—unless it affects the common good. It will keep you from doing anything useful. You'll be too preoccupied with what so-and-

so is doing, and why, and what they're saying, and what they're thinking, and what they're up to, and all the other things that throw you off and keep you from focusing on your own mind.

You need to avoid certain things in your train of thought: everything random, everything irrelevant. And certainly everything self-important or malicious. You need to get used to winnowing your thoughts, so that if someone says, "What are you thinking about?" you can respond at once (and truthfully) that you are thinking this or thinking that. And it would be obvious at once from your answer that your thoughts were straightforward and considerate ones—the thoughts of an unselfish person, one unconcerned with pleasure and with sensual indulgence generally, with squabbling, with slander and envy, or anything else you'd be ashamed to be caught thinking.

Someone like that—someone who refuses to put off joining the elect—is a kind of priest, a servant of the gods, in touch with what is within him and what keeps a person undefiled by pleasures, invulnerable to any pain, untouched by arrogance, unaffected by meanness, an athlete in the greatest of all contests—the struggle not to be overwhelmed by anything that happens. With what leaves us dyed indelibly by justice, welcoming wholeheartedly whatever comes—whatever we're assigned—not worrying too often, or with any selfish motive, about what other people say. Or do, or think.

He does only what is his to do, and considers constantly what the world has in store for him—doing his best, and trusting that all is *for* the best. For we carry our fate with us—and it carries us.

He keeps in mind that all rational things are related, and that to care for all human beings is part of being human. Which doesn't mean we have to share their opinions. We should listen only to those whose lives conform to nature. And the others? He bears in mind what sort of people they are—both at home and abroad, by night as well as day—and who they spend their time with. And he cares nothing for their praise—men who can't even meet their own standards.

5. How to act:

> Never under compulsion, out of selfishness, without forethought, with misgivings.
>
> Don't gussy up your thoughts.
>
> No surplus words or unnecessary actions.
>
> Let the spirit in you represent a man, an adult, a citizen, a Roman, a ruler. Taking up his post like a soldier and patiently awaiting his recall from life. Needing no oath or witness.
>
> Cheerfulness. Without requiring other people's help. Or serenity supplied by others.
>
> To stand up straight—not straightened.

6. If, at some point in your life, you should come across anything better than justice, honesty, self-control, courage—than a mind satisfied that it has succeeded in enabling you to act rationally, and satisfied to accept what's beyond its control—if you find anything better than that, embrace it without reservations—it must be an extraordinary thing indeed—and enjoy it to the full.

But if nothing presents itself that's superior to the spirit that lives within—the one that has subordinated individual desires to itself, that discriminates among impressions, that has broken free of physical temptations (as Socrates used to say), and subordinated itself to the gods, and looks out for human beings' welfare—if you find that there's nothing more important or valuable than that...

...then don't make room for anything but it—for anything that might lead you astray, tempt you off the road, and leave you unable to devote yourself completely to achieving the goodness that is uniquely yours. It would be wrong for anything to stand between you and attaining goodness—as a rational being and a citizen. Anything at all: the applause of the crowd, high office, wealth, or self-indulgence. All of them might seem to be compatible with it—for a while. But suddenly they control us and sweep us away.

So make your choice straightforwardly, once and for all, and stick to it. Choose what's best.

—Best is what benefits *me.*

As a rational being? Then follow through. Or just as an animal? Then say so and stand your ground without making a show of it. (Just make sure you've done your homework first.)

7. Never regard something as doing you good if it makes you betray a trust, or lose your sense of shame, or makes you show hatred, suspicion, ill will, or hypocrisy, or a desire for things best done behind closed doors. If you can privilege your own mind, your guiding spirit and your reverence for its powers, that should keep you clear of dramatics, of wailing and gnashing of teeth. You won't need solitude—or a cast of thousands, either. Above all, you'll be free of fear and desire. And how long your body will contain the soul that inhabits it will cause you not a moment's worry. If it's time for you to go, leave willingly—as you would to accomplish anything that can be done with grace and honor. And concentrate on this, your whole life long: for your mind to be in the right state—the state a rational, civic mind should be in.

8. The mind of one set straight and purified: no pus, no dirt, no scabs.

And not a life cut short by death, like an actor who stops before the play is done, the plot wound up.

Neither servility nor arrogance. Neither cringing nor disdain. Neither excuses nor evasions.

9. Your ability to control your thoughts—treat it with respect. It's all that protects your mind from false perceptions—false to your nature, and that of all rational beings. It's what makes thoughtfulness possible, and affection for other people, and submission to the divine.

10. Forget everything else. Keep hold of this alone and remember it: Each of us lives only now, this brief instant. The rest has been lived already, or is impossible to see. The span we live is small—small as the corner of the earth in which we live it. Small as even the greatest renown, passed from mouth to mouth by short-lived stick figures, ignorant alike of themselves and those long dead.

11. To the stand-bys above, add this one: always to define whatever it is we perceive—to trace its outline—so we can see what it really is: its substance. Stripped bare. As a whole. Unmodified. And to call it by its name—the thing itself and its components, to which it will eventually return. Nothing is so conducive to spiritual growth as this capacity for logical and accurate analysis of everything that happens to us. To look at it in such a way that we understand what need it fulfills, and in what kind of world. And its value to that world as a whole and to man in particular—as a citizen of that higher city, of which all other cities are mere households.

What is it—this thing that now forces itself on my notice? What is it made up of? How long was it designed to last? And what qualities do I need to bring to bear on it—tranquillity, courage, honesty, trustworthiness, straightforwardness, independence or what?

So in each case you need to say: "This is due to God." Or: "This is due to the interweavings and intertwinings of fate, to coincidence or chance." Or: "This is due to a human being. Someone of the same race, the same birth, the same society, but who doesn't know what nature requires of him. But I do. And so I'll treat them as the law that binds us—the law of nature—requires. With kindness and with justice.

And in inconsequential things? I'll do my best to treat them as they deserve."

12. If you do the job in a principled way, with diligence, energy and patience, if you keep yourself free of distractions, and keep the spirit inside you undamaged, as if you might have to give it back at any moment—

If you can embrace this without fear or expectation—can find fulfillment in what you're doing now, as Nature intended, and in superhuman truthfulness (every word, every utterance)—then your life will be happy.

No one can prevent that.

13. Doctors keep their scalpels and other instruments handy, for emergencies. Keep your philosophy ready too—ready to understand heaven and earth. In everything you do, even the smallest thing, remember the chain that links them. Nothing earthly succeeds by ignoring heaven, nothing heavenly by ignoring the earth.

14. Stop drifting. You're not going to re-read your *Brief Comments,* your *Deeds of the Ancient Greeks and Romans,* the commonplace books you saved for your old age. Sprint for the finish. Write off your hopes, and if your well-being matters to you, be your own savior while you can.

15. They don't realize how much is included in *stealing, sowing, buying, resting, seeing to business* (not with the eyes, but another kind of sight).

16. Body. Soul. Mind.
   Sensations: the body.
   Desires: the soul.
   Reasoning: the mind.

To experience sensations: even grazing beasts do that. To let your desires control you: even wild animals do that—and rutting humans, and tyrants (from Phalaris to Nero...).

To make your mind your guide to what seems best: even people who deny the gods do that. Even people who betray their country. Even people who do <...> behind closed doors.

If all the rest is common coin, then what is unique to the good man?

To welcome with affection what is sent by fate. Not to stain or disturb the spirit within him with a mess of false beliefs. Instead, to preserve it faithfully, by calmly obeying God—saying nothing untrue, doing nothing unjust. And if the others don't acknowledge it—this life lived with simplicity, humility, cheerfulness—he doesn't resent them for it, and isn't deterred from following the road where it leads: to the end of life. An end to be approached in purity, in serenity, in acceptance, in peaceful unity with what must be.

BOOK 4

1. Our inward power, when it obeys nature, reacts to events by accommodating itself to what it faces—to what is possible. It needs no specific material. It pursues its own aims as circumstances allow; it turns obstacles into fuel. As a fire overwhelms what would have quenched a lamp. What's thrown on top of the conflagration is absorbed, consumed by it—and makes it burn still higher.

2. No random actions, none not based on underlying principles.

3. People try to get away from it all—to the country, to the beach, to the mountains. You always wish that you could too. Which is idiotic: you can get away from it anytime you like.

By going within.

Nowhere you can go is more peaceful—more free of interruptions—than your own soul. Especially if you have other things to rely on. An instant's recollection and there it is: complete tranquillity. And by tranquillity I mean a kind of harmony.

So keep getting away from it all—like that. Renew yourself. But keep it brief and basic. A quick visit should be enough to ward off all < . . . > and send you back ready to face what awaits you.

What's there to complain about? People's misbehavior? But take into consideration:

- that rational beings exist for one another;
- that doing what's right sometimes requires patience;
- that no one does the wrong thing deliberately;

• and the number of people who have feuded and envied and hated and fought and died and been buried.

. . . and keep your mouth shut.

Or are you complaining about the things the world assigns you? But consider the two options: Providence or atoms. And all the arguments for seeing the world as a city.

Or is it your body? Keep in mind that when the mind detaches itself and realizes its own nature, it no longer has anything to do with ordinary life—the rough and the smooth, either one. And remember all you've been taught—and accepted—about pain and pleasure.

Or is it your reputation that's bothering you? But look at how soon we're all forgotten. The abyss of endless time that swallows it all. The emptiness of all those applauding hands. The people who praise us—how capricious they are, how arbitrary. And the tiny region in which it all takes place. The whole earth a point in space— and most of it uninhabited. How many people there will be to admire you, and who they are.

So keep this refuge in mind: the back roads of your self. Above all, no strain and no stress. Be straightforward. Look at things like a man, like a human being, like a citizen, like a mortal. And among the things you turn to, these two:

i. That things have no hold on the soul. They stand there unmoving, outside it. Disturbance comes only from within— from our own perceptions.
ii. That everything you see will soon alter and cease to exist. Think of how many changes you've already seen.

"The world is nothing but change. Our life is only perception."

4. If thought is something we share, then so is reason—what makes us reasoning beings.

If so, then the reason that tells us what to do and what not to do is also shared.

And if so, we share a common law.

And thus, are fellow citizens.

And fellow citizens of something.

And in that case, our state must be the world. What other entity could all of humanity belong to? And from it—from this state that we share—come thought and reason and law.

Where else could they come from? The earth that composes me derives from earth, the water from some other element, the air from its own source, the heat and fire from theirs—since nothing comes from nothing, or returns to it.

So thought must derive from somewhere else as well.

5. Death: something like birth, a natural mystery, elements that split and recombine.

Not an embarrassing thing. Not an offense to reason, or our nature.

6. That sort of person is bound to do that. You might as well resent a fig tree for secreting juice. (Anyway, before very long you'll both be dead—dead and soon forgotten.)

7. Choose not to be harmed—and you won't feel harmed.

Don't feel harmed—and you haven't been.

8. It can ruin your life only if it ruins your character. Otherwise it cannot harm you—inside or out.

9. It was for the best. So Nature had no choice but to do it.

10. That every event is the right one. Look closely and you'll see.

Not just the right one overall, but *right*. As if someone had weighed it out with scales.

Keep looking closely like that, and embody it in your actions: goodness—what defines a good person.

Keep to it in everything you do.

11. Not what your enemy sees and hopes that you will, but what's really there.

12. Two kinds of readiness are constantly needed: (i) to do only what the *logos* of authority and law directs, with the good of human beings in mind; (ii) to reconsider your position, when someone can set you straight or convert you to his. But your conversion should always rest on a conviction that it's right, or benefits others—nothing else. Not because it's more appealing or more popular.

13. You have a mind?

—Yes.

Well, why not use it? Isn't that all you want—for it to do its job?

14. You have functioned as a part of something; you will vanish into what produced you.

Or be restored, rather.

To the *logos* from which all things spring.

By being changed.

15. Many lumps of incense on the same altar. One crumbles now, one later, but it makes no difference.

16. Now they see you as a beast, a monkey. But in a week they'll think you're a god—if you rediscover your beliefs and honor the *logos*.

17. Not to live as if you had endless years ahead of you. Death overshadows you. While you're alive and able—be good.

18. The tranquillity that comes when you stop caring what they say. Or think, or do. Only what *you* do. (Is this fair? Is this the right thing to do?)

< ... > not to be distracted by their darkness. To run straight for the finish line, unswerving.

19. People who are excited by posthumous fame forget that the people who remember them will soon die too. And those after them in turn. Until their memory, passed from one to another like a candle flame, gutters and goes out.

But suppose that those who remembered you were immortal and your memory undying. What good would it do you? And I don't just mean when you're dead, but in your own lifetime. What use is praise, except to make your lifestyle a little more comfortable?

† You're out of step—neglecting the gifts of nature to hand on someone's words in the future. †

20. Beautiful things of any kind are beautiful in themselves and sufficient to themselves. Praise is extraneous. The object of praise remains what it was—no better and no worse. This applies, I think, even to "beautiful" things in ordinary life—physical objects, artworks.

Does anything genuinely beautiful need supplementing? No more than justice does—or truth, or kindness, or humility. Are any of those improved by being praised? Or damaged by contempt? Is an emerald suddenly flawed if no one admires it? Or gold, or ivory, or purple? Lyres? Knives? Flowers? Bushes?

21. If our souls survive, how does the air find room for them—all of them—since the beginning of time?

How does the earth find room for all the bodies buried in it since the beginning of time? They linger for whatever length of time, and then, through change and decomposition, make room for others. So too with the souls that inhabit the air. They linger a little, and then are changed—diffused and kindled into fire, absorbed into the *logos* from which all things spring, and so make room for new arrivals.

One possible answer.

But we shouldn't think only of the mass of *buried* bodies. There are the ones consumed, on a daily basis, by us and by other animals. How many are swallowed up like that, entombed in the bodies of those nourished by them, and yet there is room for them all—converted into flesh and blood, transformed to air and fire.

How is the truth of this determined?

Through analysis: material and cause.

22. Not to be driven this way and that, but always to behave with justice and see things as they are.

23. To the world: Your harmony is mine. Whatever time you choose is the right time. Not late, not early.

To nature: What the turn of your seasons brings me falls like ripe fruit. All things are born from you, exist in you, return to you.

The poet says "dear city of Cecrops..." Can't you bring yourself to say "of Zeus"?

24. "If you seek tranquillity, do less." Or (more accurately) do what's essential—what the *logos* of a social being requires, and in the requisite way. Which brings a double satisfaction: to do less, better.

Because most of what we say and do is not essential. If you can eliminate it, you'll have more time, and more tranquillity. Ask yourself at every moment, "Is this necessary?"

But we need to eliminate unnecessary assumptions as well. To eliminate the unnecessary actions that follow.

25. And then you might see what the life of the good man is like— someone content with what nature assigns him, and satisfied with being just and kind himself.

26. You've seen that. Now look at this.

Don't be disturbed. Uncomplicate yourself.

Someone has done wrong... to himself.

Something happens to you. Good. It was meant for you by nature, woven into the pattern from the beginning.

Life is short. That's all there is to say. Get what you can from the present—thoughtfully, justly.

Unrestrained moderation.

27. An ordered world or a mishmash. But still an order. Can there be order within you and not in everything else? In things so different, so dispersed, so intertwined?

28. Character: dark, womanish, obstinate. Wolf, sheep, child, fool, cheat, buffoon, salesman, tyrant.

29. Alien: (n.) one who doesn't know what the world contains. Or how it operates.

Fugitive: (n.) one who evades his obligations to others.

Blind: (adj.) one who keeps the eyes of his mind shut tight.

Poor: (adj.) requiring others; not having the necessities of life in one's own possession.

Rebel: (n.) one who is rebellious, one who withdraws from the *logos* of Nature because he resents its workings. (It produced you; now it produces this.)

Schismatic: (n.) one who separates his own soul from others with the *logos.* They should be one.

30. A philosopher without clothes and one without books. "I have nothing to eat," says he, as he stands there half-naked, "but I subsist on the *logos.*" And with nothing to read, I subsist on it too.

31. Love the discipline you know, and let it support you. Entrust everything willingly to the gods, and then make your way through life—no one's master and no one's slave.

32. The age of Vespasian, for example. People doing the exact same things: marrying, raising children, getting sick, dying, waging war, throwing parties, doing business, farming, flattering, boasting, distrusting, plotting, hoping others will die, complaining about their own lives, falling in love, putting away money, seeking high office and power.

And that life they led is nowhere to be found.

Or the age of Trajan. The exact same things. And that life too—gone.

Survey the records of other eras. And see how many others gave their all and soon died and decomposed into the elements that formed them.

But most of all, run through the list of those you knew yourself. Those who worked in vain, who failed to do what they should have—what they should have remained fixed on and found satisfaction in.

A key point to bear in mind: The value of attentiveness varies in proportion to its object. You're better off not giving the small things more time than they deserve.

33. Words once in common use now sound archaic. And the names of the famous dead as well: Camillus, Caeso, Volesus, Dentatus... Scipio and Cato... Augustus... Hadrian and Antoninus, and...

Everything fades so quickly, turns into legend, and soon oblivion covers it.

And those are the ones who shone. The rest—"unknown, unasked-for" a minute after death. What is "eternal" fame? Emptiness.

Then what should we work for?

Only this: proper understanding; unselfish action; truthful speech. A resolve to accept whatever happens as necessary and familiar, flowing like water from that same source and spring.

34. Hand yourself over to Clotho voluntarily, and let her spin you into whatever she pleases.

35. Everything transitory—the knower and the known.

36. Constant awareness that everything is born from change. The knowledge that there is nothing nature loves more than to alter what exists and make new things like it. All that exists is the seed of what will emerge from it. You think the only seeds are the ones that make plants or children? Go deeper.

37. On the verge of dying and still weighed down, still turbulent, still convinced external things can harm you, still rude to other people, still not acknowledging the truth: that wisdom is justice.

38. Look into their minds, at what the wise do and what they don't.

39. Nothing that goes on in anyone else's mind can harm you. Nor can the shifts and changes in the world around you.

   —Then where is harm to be found?

   In your capacity to see it. Stop doing that and everything will be fine. Let the part of you that makes that judgment keep quiet even if the body it's attached to is stabbed or burnt, or stinking with pus, or consumed by cancer. Or to put it another way: It needs to realize that what happens to everyone—bad and good alike—is neither good nor bad. That what happens in every life—lived naturally or not—is neither natural nor unnatural.

40. The world as a living being—one nature, one soul. Keep that in mind. And how everything feeds into that single experience, moves with a single motion. And how everything helps produce everything else. Spun and woven together.

41. "A little wisp of soul carrying a corpse."—Epictetus.

42. There is nothing bad in undergoing change—or good in emerging from it.

43. Time is a river, a violent current of events, glimpsed once and already carried past us, and another follows and is gone.

44. Everything that happens is as simple and familiar as the rose in spring, the fruit in summer: disease, death, blasphemy, conspiracy . . . everything that makes stupid people happy or angry.

45. What follows coheres with what went before. Not like a random catalogue whose order is imposed upon it arbitrarily, but logically connected. And just as what exists is ordered and harmonious, what comes into being betrays an order too. Not a mere sequence, but an astonishing concordance.

46. Remember Heraclitus: "When earth dies, it becomes water; water, air; air, fire; and back to the beginning."

"Those who have forgotten where the road leads."

"They are at odds with what is all around them"—the all-directing *logos*. And "they find alien what they meet with every day."

"Our words and actions should not be like those of sleepers" (for we act and speak in dreams as well) "or of children copying their parents"—doing and saying only what we have been told.

47. Suppose that a god announced that you were going to die tomorrow "or the day after." Unless you were a complete coward you wouldn't kick up a fuss about which day it was—what difference could it make? Now recognize that the difference between years from now and tomorrow is just as small.

48. Don't let yourself forget how many doctors have died, after furrowing their brows over how many deathbeds. How many astrologers, after pompous forecasts about others' ends. How many philosophers, after endless disquisitions on death and immortality. How many warriors, after inflicting thousands of casualties themselves. How many tyrants, after abusing the power of life and death atrociously, as if they were themselves immortal.

How many whole cities have met their end: Helike, Pompeii, Herculaneum, and countless others.

And all the ones you know yourself, one after another. One who laid out another for burial, and was buried himself, and then the man who buried him—all in the same short space of time.

In short, know this: Human lives are brief and trivial. Yesterday a blob of semen; tomorrow embalming fluid, ash.

To pass through this brief life as nature demands. To give it up without complaint.

Like an olive that ripens and falls.

Praising its mother, thanking the tree it grew on.

49. To be like the rock that the waves keep crashing over. It stands unmoved and the raging of the sea falls still around it.

49a. —It's unfortunate that this has happened.

No. It's fortunate that this has happened and I've remained unharmed by it—not shattered by the present or frightened of the future. It could have happened to anyone. But not everyone could have remained unharmed by it. Why treat the one as a misfortune rather than the other as fortunate? Can you really call something a misfortune that doesn't violate human nature? Or do you think something that's not against nature's will can violate it? But you know what its will is. Does what's happened keep you from acting with justice, generosity, self-control, sanity, prudence, honesty, humility, straightforwardness, and all the other qualities that allow a person's nature to fulfill itself?

So remember this principle when something threatens to cause you pain: the thing itself was no misfortune at all; to endure it and prevail is great good fortune.

50. A trite but effective tactic against the fear of death: think of the list of people who had to be pried away from life. What did they gain by dying old? In the end, they all sleep six feet under—Caedi-

cianus, Fabius, Julian, Lepidus, and all the rest. They buried their contemporaries, and were buried in turn.

Our lifetime is so brief. And to live it out in these circumstances, among these people, in this body? Nothing to get excited about. Consider the abyss of time past, the infinite future. Three days of life or three generations: what's the difference?

51. Take the shortest route, the one that nature planned—to speak and act in the healthiest way. Do that, and be free of pain and stress, free of all calculation and pretension.

BOOK 5

1. At dawn, when you have trouble getting out of bed, tell yourself: "I have to go to work—as a human being. What do I have to complain of, if I'm going to do what I was born for—the things I was brought into the world to do? Or is *this* what I was created for? To huddle under the blankets and stay warm?

—But it's nicer here....

So you were born to feel "nice"? Instead of doing things and experiencing them? Don't you see the plants, the birds, the ants and spiders and bees going about their individual tasks, putting the world in order, as best they can? And you're not willing to do your job as a human being? Why aren't you running to do what your nature demands?

—But we have to sleep sometime....

Agreed. But nature set a limit on that—as it did on eating and drinking. And you're over the limit. You've had more than enough of that. But not of working. There you're still below your quota.

You don't love yourself enough. Or you'd love your nature too, and what it demands of you. People who love what they do wear themselves down doing it, they even forget to wash or eat. Do you have less respect for your own nature than the engraver does for engraving, the dancer for the dance, the miser for money or the social climber for status? When they're really possessed by what they do, they'd rather stop eating and sleeping than give up practicing their arts.

Is helping others less valuable to you? Not worth your effort?

2. To shrug it all off and wipe it clean—every annoyance and distraction—and reach utter stillness.

Child's play.

3. If an action or utterance is appropriate, then it's appropriate for you. Don't be put off by other people's comments and criticism. If it's right to say or do it, then it's the right thing for you to do or say.

The others obey their own lead, follow their own impulses. Don't be distracted. Keep walking. Follow your own nature, and follow Nature—along the road they share.

4. I walk through what is natural, until the time comes to sink down and rest. To entrust my last breath to the source of my daily breathing, fall on the source of my father's seed, of my mother's blood, of my nurse's milk. Of my daily food and drink through all these years. What sustains my footsteps, and the use I make of it— the many uses.

5. No one could ever accuse you of being quick-witted.

All right, but there are plenty of other things you can't claim you "haven't got in you." Practice the virtues you *can* show: honesty, gravity, endurance, austerity, resignation, abstinence, patience, sincerity, moderation, seriousness, high-mindedness. Don't you see how much you have to offer—beyond excuses like "can't"? And yet you still settle for less.

Or is it some inborn condition that makes you whiny and grasping and obsequious, makes you complain about your body and curry favor and show off and leaves you so turbulent inside?

No. You could have broken free a long way back. And then you would have been only a little slow. "Not so quick on the uptake."

And you need to work on that as well—that slowness. Not something to be ignored, let alone to prize.

6. Some people, when they do someone a favor, are always looking for a chance to call it in. And some aren't, but they're still aware of it—still regard it as a debt. But others don't even do that. They're like a vine that produces grapes without looking for anything in return.

A horse at the end of the race...

A dog when the hunt is over...

A bee with its honey stored...

And a human being after helping others.

They don't make a fuss about it. They just go on to something else, as the vine looks forward to bearing fruit again in season.

We should be like that. Acting almost unconsciously.

—Yes. Except conscious of it. Because it's characteristic of social beings that they see themselves as acting socially. And expect their neighbors to see it too!

That's true. But you're misunderstanding me. You'll wind up like the people I mentioned before, misled by plausible reasoning. But if you make an effort to understand what I'm saying, then you won't need to worry about neglecting your social duty.

7. Prayer of the Athenians:

> Zeus, rain down, rain down
> On the land and fields of Athens.

Either no prayers at all—or one as straightforward as that.

8. Just as you overhear people saying that "the doctor prescribed such-and-such for him" (like riding, or cold baths, or walking bare-

foot...), say this: "Nature prescribed illness for him." Or blindness. Or the loss of a limb. Or whatever. There "prescribed" means something like "ordered, so as to further his recovery." And so too here. What happens to each of us is ordered. It furthers our destiny.

And when we describe things as "taking place," we're talking like builders, who say that blocks in a wall or a pyramid "take their place" in the structure, and fit together in a harmonious pattern.

For there is a single harmony. Just as the world forms a single body comprising all bodies, so fate forms a single purpose, comprising all purposes. Even complete illiterates acknowledge it when they say that something "brought on" this or that. Brought on, yes. Or prescribed it. And in that case, let's accept it—as we accept what the doctor prescribes. It may not always be pleasant, but we embrace it—because we want to get well. Look at the accomplishment of nature's plans in that light—the way you look at your own health—and accept what happens (even if it seems hard to accept). Accept it because of what it leads to: the good health of the world, and the well-being and prosperity of Zeus himself, who would not have brought this on anyone unless it brought benefit to the world as a whole. No nature would do that—bring something about that wasn't beneficial to what it governed.

So there are two reasons to embrace what happens. One is that it's happening to *you*. It was prescribed for you, and it pertains to you. The thread was spun long ago, by the oldest cause of all.

The other reason is that what happens to an individual is a cause of well-being in what directs the world—of its well-being, its fulfillment, of its very existence, even. Because the whole is damaged if you cut away anything—anything at all—from its continuity and its coherence. Not only its parts, but its purposes. And that's what you're doing when you complain: hacking and destroying.

9. Not to feel exasperated, or defeated, or despondent because your days aren't packed with wise and moral actions. But to get back up when you fail, to celebrate behaving like a human—however imperfectly—and fully embrace the pursuit that you've embarked on.

And not to think of philosophy as your instructor, but as the sponge and egg white that relieve ophthalmia—as a soothing ointment, a warm lotion. Not showing off your obedience to the *logos*, but resting in it. Remember: philosophy requires only what your nature already demands. What you've been after is something else again—something unnatural.

—But what could be preferable?

That's exactly how pleasure traps us, isn't it? Wouldn't magnanimity be preferable? Or freedom? Honesty? Prudence? Piety? And is there anything preferable to thought itself—to logic, to understanding? Think of their surefootedness. Their fluent stillness.

10. Things are wrapped in such a veil of mystery that many good philosophers have found it impossible to make sense of them. Even the Stoics have trouble. Any assessment we make is subject to alteration—just as we are ourselves.

Look closely at them—how impermanent they are, how meaningless. Things that a pervert can own, a whore, a thief.

Then look at the way the people around you behave. Even the best of them are hard to put up with—not to mention putting up with yourself. In such deep darkness, such a sewer—in the flux of material, of time, of motion and things moved—I don't know what there is to value or to work for.

Quite the contrary. We need to comfort ourselves and wait for dissolution. And not get impatient in the meantime, but take refuge in these two things:

  i. Nothing can happen to me that isn't natural.
  ii. I can keep from doing anything that God and my own spirit
  don't approve. No one can force me to.

11. What am I doing with my soul?
Interrogate yourself, to find out what inhabits your so-called
mind and what kind of soul you have now. A child's soul, an ado-
lescent's, a woman's? A tyrant's soul? The soul of a predator—or its
prey?

12. Another way to grasp what ordinary people mean by "goods":
Suppose you took certain things as touchstones of goodness:
prudence, self-control, justice, and courage, say. If you understood
"goods" as meaning those, you wouldn't be able to follow that line
about "so many goods...." It wouldn't make any sense to you.
Whereas if you'd internalized the conventional meaning, you'd be
able to follow it perfectly. You'd have no trouble seeing the author's
meaning and why it was funny.
  Which shows that most people do acknowledge a distinction.
Otherwise we wouldn't recognize the first sense as jarring and
reject it automatically, whereas we accept the second—the one
referring to wealth and the benefits of celebrity and high living—as
amusing and apropos.
  Now go a step further. Ask yourself whether we should accept
as goods—and should value—the things we have to think of to have
the line make sense—the ones whose abundance leaves their owner
with "...no place to shit."

13. I am made up of substance and what animates it, and neither
one can ever stop existing, any more than it began to. Every portion

of me will be reassigned as another portion of the world, and that in turn transformed into another. Ad infinitum.

I was produced through one such transformation, and my parents too, and so on back. Ad infinitum.

N.B.: Still holds good, even if the world goes through recurrent cycles.

14. The *logos* and its employment are forces sufficient for themselves and for their works. They start from their own beginning, they proceed to the appointed end. We call such activities "directed," from the directness of their course.

15. Nothing pertains to human beings except what defines us as human. No other things can be demanded of us. They aren't proper to human nature, nor is it incomplete without them. It follows that they are not our goal, or what helps us reach it—the good. If any of them were proper to us, it would be improper to disdain or resist it. Nor would we admire people who show themselves immune to it. If the things themselves were good, it could hardly be good to give them up. But in reality the more we deny ourselves such things (and things like them)—or are deprived of them involuntarily, even—the better we become.

16. The things you think about determine the quality of your mind. Your soul takes on the color of your thoughts. Color it with a run of thoughts like these:

    i. Anywhere you can lead your life, you can lead a good one.
      —Lives are led at court. . . .
      Then good ones can be.
    ii. Things gravitate toward what they were intended for.
      What things gravitate toward is their goal.

A thing's goal is what benefits it—its good.

A rational being's good is unselfishness. What we were born for. That's nothing new. Remember? Lower things for the sake of higher ones, and higher ones for one another. Things that have consciousness are higher than those that don't. And those with the *logos* still higher.

17. It is crazy to want what is impossible. And impossible for the wicked not to do so.

18. Nothing happens to anyone that he can't endure. The same thing happens to other people, and they weather it unharmed—out of sheer obliviousness or because they want to display "character." Is wisdom really so much weaker than ignorance and vanity?

19. Things have no hold on the soul. They have no access to it, cannot move or direct it. It is moved and directed by itself alone. It takes the things before it and interprets them as it sees fit.

20. In a sense, people are our proper occupation. Our job is to do them good and put up with them.

But when they obstruct our proper tasks, they become irrelevant to us—like sun, wind, animals. Our actions may be impeded by them, but there can be no impeding our intentions or our dispositions. Because we can accommodate and adapt. The mind adapts and converts to its own purposes the obstacle to our acting.

The impediment to action advances action.

What stands in the way becomes the way.

21. Honor that which is greatest in the world—that on whose business all things are employed and by whom they are governed.

And honor what is greatest in yourself: the part that shares its nature with that power. All things—in you as well—are employed about its business, and your life is governed by it.

22. If it does not harm the community, it does not harm its members.

When you think you've been injured, apply this rule: If the community isn't injured by it, neither am I. And if it is, anger is not the answer. Show the offender where he went wrong.

23. Keep in mind how fast things pass by and are gone—those that are now, and those to come. Existence flows past us like a river: the "what" is in constant flux, the "why" has a thousand variations. Nothing is stable, not even what's right here. The infinity of past and future gapes before us—a chasm whose depths we cannot see.

So it would take an idiot to feel self-importance or distress. Or any indignation, either. As if the things that irritate us lasted.

24. Remember:
Matter. How tiny your share of it.
Time. How brief and fleeting your allotment of it.
Fate. How small a role you play in it.

25. So other people hurt me? That's their problem. Their character and actions are not mine. What is done to me is ordained by nature, what I do by my own.

26. The mind is the ruler of the soul. It should remain unstirred by agitations of the flesh—gentle and violent ones alike. Not mingling with them, but fencing itself off and keeping those feelings in their place. When they make their way into your thoughts, through the

sympathetic link between mind and body, don't try to resist the sensation. The sensation is natural. But don't let the mind start in with judgments, calling it "good" or "bad."

27. "To live with the gods." And to do that is to show them that your soul accepts what it is given and does what the spirit requires— the spirit God gave each of us to lead and guide us, a fragment of himself. Which is our mind, our *logos*.

28. Don't be irritated at people's smell or bad breath. What's the point? With that mouth, with those armpits, they're going to produce that odor.

—But they have a brain! Can't they figure it out? Can't they recognize the problem?

So you have a brain as well. Good for you. Then use your logic to awaken his. Show him. Make him realize it. If he'll listen, then you'll have solved the problem. Without anger.

28a. Neither player-king nor prostitute.

29. You can live here as you expect to live there.

And if they won't let you, you can depart life now and forfeit nothing. If the smoke makes me cough, I can leave. What's so hard about that?

Until things reach that point, I'm free. No one can keep me from doing what I want. And I want what is proper to rational beings, living together.

30. The world's intelligence is not selfish.

It created lower things for the sake of higher ones, and attuned the higher ones to one another. Look how it subordinates, how it connects, how it assigns each thing what each deserves, and brings the better things into alignment.

31. How have you behaved to the gods, to your parents, to your siblings, to your wife, to your children, to your teachers, to your nurses, to your friends, to your relatives, to your slaves? Have they all had from you nothing "wrong and unworthy, either word or deed"?

Consider all that you've gone through, all that you've survived. And that the story of your life is done, your assignment complete. How many good things have you seen? How much pain and pleasure have you resisted? How many honors have you declined? How many unkind people have you been kind to?

32. Why do other souls—unskilled, untrained—disturb the soul with skill and understanding?

—And which is that?

The one that knows the beginning and the end, and knows the *logos* that runs through all things and that assigns to all a place, each in its allotted span, throughout the whole of time.

33. Soon you'll be ashes, or bones. A mere name, at most—and even that is just a sound, an echo. The things we want in life are empty, stale, and trivial. Dogs snarling at each other. Quarreling children—laughing and then bursting into tears a moment later. Trust, shame, justice, truth—"gone from the earth and only found in heaven."

Why are you still here? Sensory objects are shifting and unstable; our senses dim and easily deceived; the soul itself a decoction of the blood; fame in a world like this is worthless.

—And so?

Wait for it patiently—annihilation or metamorphosis.

—And until that time comes—what?

Honor and revere the gods, treat human beings as they deserve, be tolerant with others and strict with yourself. Remember, nothing belongs to you but your flesh and blood—and nothing else is under your control.

34. You can lead an untroubled life provided you can grow, can think and act systematically.

Two characteristics shared by gods and men (and every rational creature):

  i. Not to let others hold you back.
  ii. To locate goodness in thinking and doing the right thing, and to limit your desires to that.

35. If:

- this evil is not of my doing,
- nor the result of it,
- and the community is not endangered,
  why should it bother me?

Where's the danger for the community?

36. Not to be overwhelmed by what you imagine, but just do what you can and should. And if < ... > suffer in inessentials, not to treat that as a defeat. (Bad habit.)

Like the old man asking for the orphan's toy on the way out— even though he knew that's all it was. Like that.

36a. † Up on the platform. †

Have you forgotten what's what?

—I know, but it was important to them.

And so you have to be an idiot as well?

37. I was once a fortunate man but at some point fortune abandoned me.

But true good fortune is what you make for yourself. Good fortune: good character, good intentions, and good actions.

BOOK 6

1. Nature is pliable, obedient. And the *logos* that governs it has no reason to do evil. It knows no evil, does none, and causes harm to nothing. It dictates all beginnings and all endings.

2. Just that you do the right thing. The rest doesn't matter.
   Cold or warm.
   Tired or well-rested.
   Despised or honored.
   Dying... or busy with other assignments.

Because dying, too, is one of our assignments in life. There as well: "to do what needs doing."

3. Look inward. Don't let the true nature or value of anything elude you.

4. Before long, all existing things will be transformed, to rise like smoke (assuming all things become one), or be dispersed in fragments.

5. The *logos* knows where it stands, and what it has to do, and what it has to work with.

6. The best revenge is not to be like that.

7. To move from one unselfish action to another with God in mind.

Only there, delight and stillness.

8. The mind is that which is roused and directed by itself. It makes of itself what it chooses. It makes what it chooses of its own experience.

9. Everything is brought about by nature, not by anything beyond it, or within it, or apart from it.

10. (i) Mixture, interaction, dispersal; or (ii) unity, order, design.

Suppose (i): Why would I want to live in disorder and confusion? Why would I care about anything except the eventual "dust to dust"? And why would I feel any anxiety? Dispersal is certain, whatever I do.

Or suppose (ii): Reverence. Serenity. Faith in the power responsible.

11. When jarred, unavoidably, by circumstances, revert at once to yourself, and don't lose the rhythm more than you can help. You'll have a better grasp of the harmony if you keep on going back to it.

12. If you had a stepmother and a real mother, you would pay your respects to your stepmother, yes . . . but it's your real mother you'd go home to.

The court . . . and philosophy: Keep returning to it, to rest in its embrace. It's all that makes the court—and you—endurable.

13. Like seeing roasted meat and other dishes in front of you and suddenly realizing: This is a dead fish. A dead bird. A dead pig. Or that this noble vintage is grape juice, and the purple robes are sheep

wool dyed with shellfish blood. Or making love—something rubbing against your penis, a brief seizure and a little cloudy liquid.

Perceptions like that—latching onto things and piercing through them, so we see what they really are. That's what we need to do all the time—all through our lives when things lay claim to our trust—to lay them bare and see how pointless they are, to strip away the legend that encrusts them.

Pride is a master of deception: when you think you're occupied in the weightiest business, that's when he has you in his spell.

(Compare Crates on Xenocrates.)

14. Things ordinary people are impressed by fall into the categories of things that are held together by simple physics (like stones or wood), or by natural growth (figs, vines, olives...). Those admired by more advanced minds are held together by a living soul (flocks of sheep, herds of cows). Still more sophisticated people admire what is guided by a rational mind—not the universal mind, but one admired for its technical knowledge, or for some other skill—or just because it happens to own a lot of slaves.

But those who revere that other mind—the one we all share, as humans and as citizens—aren't interested in other things. Their focus is on the state of their own minds—to avoid all selfishness and illogic, and to work with others to achieve that goal.

15. Some things are rushing into existence, others out of it. Some of what now exists is already gone. Change and flux constantly remake the world, just as the incessant progression of time remakes eternity.

We find ourselves in a river. Which of the things around us should we value when none of them can offer a firm foothold?

Like an attachment to a sparrow: we glimpse it and it's gone.

And life itself: like the decoction of blood, the drawing in of air. We expel the power of breathing we drew in at birth (just yesterday or the day before), breathing it out like the air we exhale at each moment.

16. What is it in ourselves that we should prize?

Not just transpiration (even plants do that).
Or respiration (even beasts and wild animals breathe).
Or being struck by passing thoughts.
Or jerked like a puppet by your own impulses.
Or moving in herds.
Or eating, and relieving yourself afterwards.

Then what is to be prized?

An audience clapping? No. No more than the clacking of their tongues. Which is all that public praise amounts to—a clacking of tongues.

So we throw out other people's recognition. What's left for us to prize?

I think it's this: to do (and not do) what we were designed for. That's the goal of all trades, all arts, and what each of them aims at: that the thing they create should do what it was designed to do. The nurseryman who cares for the vines, the horse trainer, the dog breeder—this is what they aim at. And teaching and education—what else are they trying to accomplish?

So that's what we should prize. Hold on to that, and you won't be tempted to aim at anything else.

And if you can't stop prizing a lot of other things? Then you'll never be free—free, independent, imperturbable. Because you'll always be envious and jealous, afraid that people might come and take it all away from you. Plotting against those who have them—

those things you prize. People who need those things are bound to be a mess—and bound to take out their frustrations on the gods. Whereas to respect your own mind—to prize it—will leave you satisfied with your own self, well integrated into your community and in tune with the gods as well—embracing what they allot you, and what they ordain.

17. The elements move upward, downward, in all directions. The motion of virtue is different—deeper. It moves at a steady pace on a road hard to discern, and always forward.

18. The way people behave. They refuse to admire their contemporaries, the people whose lives they share. No, but to be admired by Posterity—people they've never met and never will—that's what they set their hearts on. You might as well be upset at not being a hero to your great-grandfather.

19. Not to assume it's impossible because you find it hard. But to recognize that if it's humanly possible, you can do it too.

20. In the ring, our opponents can gouge us with their nails or butt us with their heads and leave a bruise, but we don't denounce them for it or get upset with them or regard them from then on as violent types. We just keep an eye on them after that. Not out of hatred or suspicion. Just keeping a friendly distance.

  We need to do that in other areas. We need to excuse what our sparring partners do, and just keep our distance—without suspicion or hatred.

21. If anyone can refute me—show me I'm making a mistake or looking at things from the wrong perspective—I'll gladly change.

It's the truth I'm after, and the truth never harmed anyone. What harms us is to persist in self-deceit and ignorance.

22. I do what is mine to do; the rest doesn't disturb me. The rest is inanimate, or has no *logos,* or it wanders at random and has lost the road.

23. When you deal with irrational animals, with things and circumstances, be generous and straightforward. You are rational; they are not. When you deal with fellow human beings, behave as one. They share in the *logos.* And invoke the gods regardless.

Don't worry about how long you'll go on doing this.

A single afternoon would be enough.

24. Alexander the Great and his mule driver both died and the same thing happened to both. They were absorbed alike into the life force of the world, or dissolved alike into atoms.

25. Think how much is going on inside you every second—in your soul, in your body. Why should it astonish you that so much more—everything that happens in that all-embracing unity, the world—is happening at the same time?

26. If someone asked you how to write your name, would you clench your teeth and spit out the letters one by one? If he lost his temper, would you lose yours as well? Or would you just spell out the individual letters?

Remember—your responsibilities can be broken down into individual parts as well. Concentrate on those, and finish the job methodically—without getting stirred up or meeting anger with anger.

27. How cruel—to forbid people to want what they think is good for them. And yet that's just what you won't let them do when you get angry at their misbehavior. They're drawn toward what they think is good for them.

—But it's *not* good for them.

Then show them that. Prove it to them. Instead of losing your temper.

28. Death. The end of sense-perception, of being controlled by our emotions, of mental activity, of enslavement to our bodies.

29. Disgraceful: for the soul to give up when the body is still going strong.

30. To escape imperialization—that indelible stain. It happens. Make sure you remain straightforward, upright, reverent, serious, un-adorned, an ally of justice, pious, kind, affectionate, and doing your duty with a will. Fight to be the person philosophy tried to make you.

Revere the gods; watch over human beings. Our lives are short. The only rewards of our existence here are an unstained character and unselfish acts.

Take Antoninus as your model, always. His energy in doing what was rational... his steadiness in any situation... his sense of rever-ence... his calm expression... his gentleness... his modesty... his eagerness to grasp things. And how he never let things go before he was sure he had examined them thoroughly, understood them perfectly... the way he put up with unfair criticism, without return-ing it... how he couldn't be hurried... how he wouldn't listen to informers... how reliable he was as a judge of character, and of actions... not prone to backbiting, or cowardice, or jealousy, or empty rhetoric... content with the basics—in living quarters, bedding, clothes, food, servants... how hard he worked, how much he put up with... his ability to work straight through till dusk—because of his simple diet (he didn't even need to relieve himself, except at set times)... his constancy and reliability as a friend... his tolerance of people who openly questioned his views and his delight at seeing his ideas improved on... his piety—without a trace of superstition...

So that when your time comes, your conscience will be as clear as his.

31. Awaken; return to yourself. Now, no longer asleep, knowing they were only dreams, clear-headed again, treat everything around you as a dream.

32. I am composed of a body and a soul.

Things that happen to the body are meaningless. It cannot discriminate among them.

Nothing has meaning to my mind except its own actions. Which are within its own control. And it's only the immediate ones that matter. Its past and future actions too are meaningless.

33. It's normal to feel pain in your hands and feet, if you're using your feet as feet and your hands as hands. And for a human being to feel stress is normal—if he's living a normal human life.

And if it's normal, how can it be bad?

34. Thieves, perverts, parricides, dictators: the kind of pleasures they enjoy.

35. Have you noticed how professionals will meet the man on the street halfway but without compromising the *logos* of their trade?

Should we as humans feel less responsibility to our *logos* than builders or pharmacists do? A *logos* we share with the divine?

36. Asia and Europe: distant recesses of the universe.
   The ocean: a drop of water.
   Mount Athos: a molehill.
   The present: a split second in eternity.
   Minuscule, transitory, insignificant.

36a. Everything derives from it—that universal mind—either as effect or consequence. The lion's jaws, the poisonous substances, and every harmful thing—from thorns to mud . . . are by-products of the good and beautiful. So don't look at them as alien to what you revere, but focus on the source that all things spring from.

37. If you've seen the present then you've seen everything—as it's been since the beginning, as it will be forever. The same substance, the same form. All of it.

38. Keep reminding yourself of the way things are connected, of their relatedness. All things are implicated in one another and in sympathy with each other. This event is the consequence of some other one. Things push and pull on each other, and breathe together, and are one.

39. The things ordained for you—teach yourself to be at one with those. And the people who share them with you—treat them with love.
   With *real* love.

40. Implements, tools, equipment. If they do what they were designed for, then they work. Even if the person who designed them is miles away.

But with naturally occurring things, the force that designed them is present within them and remains there. Which is why we owe it special reverence, with the recognition that if you live and act as it dictates, then everything in you is intelligently ordered. Just as everything in the world is.

41. You take things you don't control and define them as "good" or "bad." And so of course when the "bad" things happen, or the "good" ones don't, you blame the gods and feel hatred for the people responsible—or those you decide to make responsible. Much of our bad behavior stems from trying to apply those criteria. If we limited "good" and "bad" to our own actions, we'd have no call to challenge God, or to treat other people as enemies.

42. All of us are working on the same project. Some consciously, with understanding; some without knowing it. (I think this is what Heraclitus meant when he said that "those who sleep are also hard at work"—that they too collaborate in what happens.) Some of us work in one way, and some in others. And those who complain and try to obstruct and thwart things—they help as much as anyone. The world needs them as well.

So make up your mind who you'll choose to work with. The force that directs all things will make good use of you regardless—will put you on its payroll and set you to work. But make sure it's not the job Chrysippus speaks of: the bad line in the play, put there for laughs.

43. Does the sun try to do the rain's work? Or Asclepius Demeter's? And what about each of the stars—different, yet working in common?

44. If the gods have made decisions about me and the things that happen to me, then they were good decisions. (It's hard to picture a god who makes bad ones.) And why would they expend their energies on causing me harm? What good would it do them—or the world, which is their primary concern?

And if they haven't made decisions about me as an individual, they certainly have about the general welfare. And anything that follows from that is something I have to welcome and embrace.

And if they make no decisions, about anything—and it's blasphemous even to think so (because if so, then let's stop sacrificing, praying, swearing oaths, and doing all the other things we do, believing the whole time that the gods are right here with us)—if they decide nothing about our lives . . . well, *I* can still make decisions. Can still consider what it's to my benefit to do. And what benefits anyone is to do what his own nature requires. And mine is rational. Rational and civic.

My city and state are Rome—as Antoninus. But as a human being? The world. So for me, "good" can only mean what's good for both communities.

45. Whatever happens to you is for the good of the world. That would be enough right there. But if you look closely you'll generally notice something else as well: whatever happens to a single person is for the good of others. (Good in the ordinary sense—as the world defines it.)

46. Just as the arena and the other spectacles weary you—you've seen them all before—and the repetition grates on your nerves, so too with life. The same things, the same causes, on all sides.

How much longer?

47. Keep this constantly in mind: that all sorts of people have died—all professions, all nationalities. Follow the thought all the way down to Philistion, Phoebus, and Origanion. Now extend it to other species.

We have to go there too, where all of them have already gone:

...the eloquent and the wise—Heraclitus, Pythagoras, Socrates...
...the heroes of old, the soldiers and kings who followed them...
...Eudoxus, Hipparchus, Archimedes...
...the smart, the generous, the hardworking, the cunning, the selfish...
...and even Menippus and his cohorts, who laughed at the whole brief, fragile business.

All underground for a long time now.

And what harm does it do them? Or the others either—the ones whose names we don't even know?

The only thing that isn't worthless: to live this life out truthfully and rightly. And be patient with those who don't.

48. When you need encouragement, think of the qualities the people around you have: this one's energy, that one's modesty, another's generosity, and so on. Nothing is as encouraging as when virtues are visibly embodied in the people around us, when we're practically showered with them.

It's good to keep this in mind.

49. It doesn't bother you that you weigh only x or y pounds and not three hundred. Why should it bother you that you have only x or y years to live and not more? You accept the limits placed on your body. Accept those placed on your time.

50. Do your best to convince them. But act on your own, if justice requires it. If met with force, then fall back on acceptance and peaceability. Use the setback to practice other virtues.

Remember that our efforts are subject to circumstances; you weren't aiming to do the impossible.

—Aiming to do what, then?

To try. And you succeeded. What you set out to do is accomplished.

51. Ambition means tying your well-being to what other people say or do.

Self-indulgence means tying it to the things that happen to you.

Sanity means tying it to your own actions.

52. You don't *have* to turn this into something. It doesn't have to upset you. Things can't shape our decisions by themselves.

53. Practice really hearing what people say. Do your best to get inside their minds.

54. What injures the hive injures the bee.

55. If the crew talked back to the captain, or patients to their doctor, then whose authority would they accept? How could the passengers be kept safe or the patient healthy?

56. All those people who came into the world with me and have already left it.

57. Honey tastes bitter to a man with jaundice. People with rabies are terrified of water. And a child's idea of beauty is a ball. Why

does that upset you? Do you think falsehood is less powerful than bile or a rabid dog?

58. No one can keep you from living as your nature requires. Nothing can happen to you that is not required by Nature.

59. The people they want to ingratiate themselves with, and the results, and the things they do in the process. How quickly it will all be erased by time. How much has been erased already.

BOOK 7

1. Evil: the same old thing.

No matter what happens, keep this in mind: It's the same old thing, from one end of the world to the other. It fills the history books, ancient and modern, and the cities, and the houses too. Nothing new at all.

Familiar, transient.

2. You cannot quench understanding unless you put out the insights that compose it. But you can rekindle those at will, like glowing coals. I can control my thoughts as necessary; then how can I be troubled? What is outside my mind means nothing to it. Absorb that lesson and your feet stand firm.

You can return to life. Look at things as you did before. And life returns.

3. Pointless bustling of processions, opera arias, herds of sheep and cattle, military exercises. A bone flung to pet poodles, a little food in the fish tank. The miserable servitude of ants, scampering of frightened mice, puppets jerked on strings.

Surrounded as we are by all of this, we need to practice acceptance. Without disdain. But remembering that our own worth is measured by what we devote our energy to.

4. Focus on what is said when you speak and on what results from each action. Know what the one aims at, and what the other means.

5. Is my intellect up to this? If so, then I'll put it to work, like a tool provided by nature. And if it isn't, then I'll turn the job over to someone who can do better—unless I have no choice.

Or I do the best I can with it, and collaborate with whoever can make use of it, to do what the community needs done. Because whatever I do—alone or with others—can aim at one thing only: what squares with those requirements.

6. So many who were remembered already forgotten, and those who remembered them long gone.

7. Don't be ashamed to need help. Like a soldier storming a wall, you have a mission to accomplish. And if you've been wounded and you need a comrade to pull you up? So what?

8. Forget the future. When and if it comes, you'll have the same resources to draw on—the same *logos.*

9. Everything is interwoven, and the web is holy; none of its parts are unconnected. They are composed harmoniously, and together they compose the world.

One world, made up of all things.

One divinity, present in them all.

One substance and one law—the *logos* that all rational beings share.

And one truth...

If this is indeed the culmination of one process, beings who share the same birth, the same *logos.*

10. All substance is soon absorbed into nature, all that animates it soon restored to the *logos,* all trace of them both soon covered over by time.

11. To a being with *logos,* an unnatural action is one that conflicts with the *logos.*

12. Straight, not straightened.

13. What is rational in different beings is related, like the individual limbs of a single being, and meant to function as a unit.

This will be clearer to you if you remind yourself: I am a single limb (*melos*) of a larger body—a rational one.

Or you could say "a part" (*meros*)—only a letter's difference. But then you're not really embracing other people. Helping them isn't yet its own reward. You're still seeing it only as The Right Thing To Do. You don't yet realize who you're really helping.

14. Let it happen, if it wants, to whatever it can happen to. And what's affected can complain about it if it wants. It doesn't hurt me unless I interpret its happening as harmful to me. I can choose not to.

15. No matter what anyone says or does, my task is to be good. Like gold or emerald or purple repeating to itself, "No matter what anyone says or does, my task is to be emerald, my color undiminished."

16. The mind doesn't get in its own way. It doesn't frighten itself into desires. If other things can scare or hurt it, let them; it won't go down that road on the basis of its own perceptions.

Let the body avoid discomfort (if it can), and if it feels it, say so. But the soul is what feels fear and pain, and what conceives of them in the first place, and it suffers nothing. Because it will never conclude that it has.

The mind in itself has no needs, except for those it creates

itself. Is undisturbed, except for its own disturbances. Knows no
obstructions, except those from within.

17. Well-being is good luck, or good character.

17a. (But what are you doing here, Perceptions? Get back to where
you came from, and good riddance. I don't need you. Yes, I know, it
was only force of habit that brought you. No, I'm not angry with
you. Just go away.)

18. Frightened of change? But what can exist without it? What's
closer to nature's heart? Can you take a hot bath and leave the fire-
wood as it was? Eat food without transforming it? Can any vital
process take place without something being changed?

Can't you see? It's just the same with you—and just as vital to
nature.

19. Carried through existence as through rushing rapids. All bodies. Which are sprung from nature and cooperate with it, as our
limbs do with each other. Time has swallowed a Chrysippus, a
Socrates and an Epictetus, many times over.

For "Epictetus" read any person, and any thing.

20. My only fear is doing something contrary to human nature—
the wrong thing, the wrong way, or at the wrong time.

21. Close to forgetting it all, close to being forgotten.

22. To feel affection for people even when they make mistakes is
uniquely human. You can do it, if you simply recognize: that they're
human too, that they act out of ignorance, against their will, and that

you'll both be dead before long. And, above all, that they haven't really hurt you. They haven't diminished your ability to choose.

23. Nature takes substance and makes a horse. Like a sculptor with wax. And then melts it down and uses the material for a tree. Then for a person. Then for something else. Each existing only briefly.

It does the container no harm to be put together, and none to be taken apart.

24. Anger in the face is unnatural. † ... † or in the end is put out for good, so that it can't be rekindled. Try to conclude its unnaturalness from that. (If even the consciousness of acting badly has gone, why go on living?)

25. Before long, nature, which controls it all, will alter everything you see and use it as material for something else—over and over again. So that the world is continually renewed.

26. When people injure you, ask yourself what good or harm they thought would come of it. If you understand that, you'll feel sympathy rather than outrage or anger. Your sense of good and evil may be the same as theirs, or near it, in which case you have to excuse them. Or your sense of good and evil may differ from theirs. In which case they're misguided and deserve your compassion. Is that so hard?

27. Treat what you don't have as nonexistent. Look at what you have, the things you value most, and think of how much you'd crave them if you didn't have them. But be careful. Don't feel such satisfaction that you start to overvalue them—that it would upset you to lose them.

28. Self-contraction: the mind's requirements are satisfied by doing what we should, and by the calm it brings us.

29. Discard your misperceptions.
    Stop being jerked like a puppet.
    Limit yourself to the present.
    Understand what happens—to you, to others.
    Analyze what exists, break it all down: material and cause.
    Anticipate your final hours.
    Other people's mistakes? Leave them to their makers.

30. To direct your thoughts to what is said. To focus the mind on what happens and what makes it happen.

31. Wash yourself clean. With simplicity, with humility, with indifference to everything but right and wrong.
    Care for other human beings. Follow God.

31a. "...all are relative," it's been said, "and in reality only atoms." It's enough to remember the first half: "all are relative." † Which is little enough. †

32. [On death:] If atoms, dispersed. If oneness, quenched or changed.

33. [On pain:] Unendurable pain brings its own end with it. Chronic pain is always endurable: the intelligence maintains serenity by cutting itself off from the body, the mind remains undiminished. And the parts that pain affects—let them speak for themselves, if they can.

34. [On Ambition:] How their minds work, the things they long for and fear. Events like piles of sand, drift upon drift—each one soon hidden by the next.

35. " 'If his mind is filled with nobility, with a grasp of all time, all existence, do you think our human life will mean much to him at all?'
" 'How could it?' he said.
" 'Or death be very frightening?'
" 'Not in the least.' "

36. "Kingship: to earn a bad reputation by good deeds."

37. Disgraceful: that the mind should control the face, should be able to shape and mold it as it pleases, but not shape and mold itself.

38. "And why should we feel anger at the world?
As if the world would notice!"

39. "May you bring joy to us and those on high."

40. "To harvest life like standing stalks of grain
Grown and cut down in turn."

41. "If I and my two children cannot move the gods
The gods must have their reasons."

42. "For what is just and good is on my side."

43. No chorus of lamentation, no hysterics.

44. "Then the only proper response for me to make is this: 'You are much mistaken, my friend, if you think that any man worth his salt cares about the risk of death and doesn't concentrate on this alone: whether what he's doing is right or wrong, and his behavior a good man's or a bad one's.' "

45. "It's like this, gentlemen of the jury: The spot where a person decides to station himself, or wherever his commanding officer stations him—well, I think that's where he ought to take his stand and face the enemy, and not worry about being killed, or about anything but doing his duty."

46. "But, my good friend, consider the possibility that nobility and virtue are not synonymous with the loss or preservation of one's life. Is it not possible that a real man should forget about living a certain number of years, and should not cling to life, but leave it up to the gods, accepting, as women say, that 'no one can escape his fate,' and turn his attention to how he can best live the life before him?"

47. To watch the courses of the stars as if you revolved with them. To keep constantly in mind how the elements alter into one another. Thoughts like this wash off the mud of life below.

48. [Plato has it right.] If you want to talk about people, you need to look down on the earth from above. Herds, armies, farms; weddings, divorces, births, deaths; noisy courtrooms, desert places; all the foreign peoples; holidays, days of mourning, market days... all mixed together, a harmony of opposites.

49. Look at the past—empire succeeding empire—and from that, extrapolate the future: the same thing. No escape from the rhythm of events.

Which is why observing life for forty years is as good as a thousand. Would you really see anything new?

50. "... Earth's offspring back to earth
But all that's born of heaven
To heaven returns again."

Either that or the cluster of atoms pulls apart and one way or another the insensible elements disperse.

51. "... with food and drink and magic spells
Seeking some novel way to frustrate death."

51a. "To labor cheerfully and so endure
The wind that blows from heaven."

52. A better wrestler. But not a better citizen, a better person, a better resource in tight places, a better forgiver of faults.

53. Wherever something can be done as the *logos* shared by gods and men dictates, there all is in order. Where there is profit because our effort is productive, because it advances in step with our nature, there we have nothing to fear.

54. Everywhere, at each moment, you have the option:

  • to accept this event with humility
  • to treat this person as he should be treated
  • to approach this thought with care, so that nothing irrational creeps in.

55. Don't pay attention to other people's minds. Look straight ahead, where nature is leading you—nature in general, through the

things that happen to you; and your own nature, through your own actions.

Everything has to do what it was made for. And other things were made for those with *logos*. In this respect as in others: lower things exist for the sake of higher ones, and higher things for one another.

Now, the main thing we were made for is to work with others.

Secondly, to resist our body's urges. Because things driven by *logos*—by thought—have the capacity for detachment—to resist impulses and sensations, both of which are merely corporeal. Thought seeks to be their master, not their subject. And so it should: they were created for its use.

And the third thing is to avoid rashness and credulity.

The mind that grasps this and steers straight ahead should be able to hold its own.

56. Think of yourself as dead. You have lived your life. Now take what's left and live it properly.

57. To love only what happens, what was destined. No greater harmony.

58. In all that happens, keep before your eyes those who experienced it before you, and felt shock and outrage and resentment at it.

And now where are they? Nowhere.

Is that what you want to be like? Instead of avoiding all these distracting assaults—leaving the alarms and flight to others—and concentrating on what you can *do* with it all?

Because you can use it, treat it as raw material. Just pay attention, and resolve to live up to your own expectations. In everything.

And when faced with a choice, remember: our business is with things that really matter.

59. Dig deep; the water—goodness—is down there. And as long as you keep digging, it will keep bubbling up.

60. What the body needs is stability. To be impervious to jolts in all it is and does. The cohesiveness and beauty that intelligence lends to the face—that's what the body needs.

But it should come without effort.

61. Not a dancer but a wrestler: waiting, poised and dug in, for sudden assaults.

62. Look at who they really are, the people whose approval you long for, and what their minds are really like. Then you won't blame the ones who make mistakes they can't help, and you won't feel a need for their approval. You will have seen the sources of both—their judgments and their actions.

63. "Against our will, our souls are cut off from truth."

Truth, yes, and justice, self-control, kindness...

Important to keep this in mind. It will make you more patient with other people.

64. For times when you feel pain:

See that it doesn't disgrace you, or degrade your intelligence—doesn't keep it from acting rationally or unselfishly.

And in most cases what Epicurus said should help: that pain is neither unbearable nor unending, as long as you keep in mind its limits and don't magnify them in your imagination.

And keep in mind too that pain often comes in disguise—as drowsiness, fever, loss of appetite.... When you're bothered by things like that, remind yourself: "I'm giving in to pain."

65. Take care that you don't treat inhumanity as it treats human beings.

66. How do we know that Telauges wasn't a better man than Socrates?

It's not enough to ask whether Socrates' death was nobler, whether he debated with the sophists more adeptly, whether he showed greater endurance by spending the night out in the cold, and when he was ordered to arrest the man from Salamis decided it was preferable to refuse, and "swaggered about the streets" (which one could reasonably doubt).

What matters is what kind of soul he had.

Whether he was satisfied to treat men with justice and the gods with reverence and didn't lose his temper unpredictably at evil done by others, didn't make himself the slave of other people's ignorance, didn't treat anything that nature did as abnormal, or put up with it as an unbearable imposition, didn't put his mind in his body's keeping.

67. Nature did not blend things so inextricably that you can't draw your own boundaries—place your own well-being in your own hands. It's quite possible to be a good man without anyone realizing it. Remember that.

And this too: you don't need much to live happily. And just because you've abandoned your hopes of becoming a great thinker or scientist, don't give up on attaining freedom, achieving humility, serving others, obeying God.

68. To live life in peace, immune to all compulsion. Let them scream whatever they want. Let animals dismember this soft flesh that covers you. How would any of that stop you from keeping your mind calm—reliably sizing up what's around you—and ready to make good use of whatever happens? So that Judgment can look the event in the eye and say, "This is what you really are, regardless of what you may look like." While Adaptability adds, "You're just what I was looking for." Because to me the present is a chance for the exercise of rational virtue—civic virtue—in short, the art that men share with gods. Both treat whatever happens as wholly natural; not novel or hard to deal with, but familiar and easily handled.

69. Perfection of character: to live your last day, every day, without frenzy, or sloth, or pretense.

70. The gods live forever and yet they don't seem annoyed at having to put up with human beings and their behavior throughout eternity. And not only put up with but actively care for them.

And you—on the verge of death—you still refuse to care for them, although you're one of them yourself.

71. It's silly to try to escape other people's faults. They are inescapable. Just try to escape your own.

72. Whenever the force that makes us rational and social encounters something that is neither, then it can reasonably regard it as inferior.

73. You've given aid and they've received it. And yet, like an idiot, you keep holding out for more: to be credited with a Good Deed, to be repaid in kind. Why?

74. No one objects to what is useful to him.

To be of use to others is natural.

Then don't object to what is useful to you—being of use.

75. Nature willed the creation of the world. Either all that exists follows logically or even those things to which the world's intelligence most directs its will are completely random.

A source of serenity in more situations than one.

BOOK 8

1. Another encouragement to humility: you can't claim to have lived your life as a philosopher—not even your whole adulthood. You can see for yourself how far you are from philosophy. And so can many others. You're tainted. It's not so easy now—to have a reputation as a philosopher. And your position is an obstacle as well.

So you know how things stand. Now forget what they think of you. Be satisfied if you can live the rest of your life, however short, as your nature demands. Focus on that, and don't let anything distract you. You've wandered all over and finally realized that you never found what you were after: how to live. Not in syllogisms, not in money, or fame, or self-indulgence. Nowhere.

—Then where is it to be found?

In doing what human nature requires.

—How?

Through first principles. Which should govern your intentions and your actions.

—What principles?

Those to do with good and evil. That nothing is good except what leads to fairness, and self-control, and courage, and free will. And nothing bad except what does the opposite.

2. For every action, ask: How does it affect me? Could I change my mind about it?

But soon I'll be dead, and the slate's empty. So this is the only question: Is it the action of a responsible being, part of society, and subject to the same decrees as God?

3. Alexander and Caesar and Pompey. Compared with Diogenes, Heraclitus, Socrates? The philosophers knew the what, the why, the how. Their minds were their own.

The others? Nothing but anxiety and enslavement.

4. You can hold your breath until you turn blue, but they'll still go on doing it.

5. The first step: Don't be anxious. Nature controls it all. And before long you'll be no one, nowhere—like Hadrian, like Augustus.

The second step: Concentrate on what you have to do. Fix your eyes on it. Remind yourself that your task is to be a good human being; remind yourself what nature demands of people. Then do it, without hesitation, and speak the truth as you see it. But with kindness. With humility. Without hypocrisy.

6. Nature's job: to shift things elsewhere, to transform them, to pick them up and move them here and there. Constant alteration. But not to worry: there's nothing new here. Everything is familiar. Even the proportions are unchanged.

7. Nature of any kind thrives on forward progress. And progress for a rational mind means not accepting falsehood or uncertainty in its perceptions, making unselfish actions its only aim, seeking and shunning only the things it has control over, embracing what nature demands of it—the nature in which it participates, as the leaf's nature does in the tree's. Except that the nature shared by the leaf is without consciousness or reason, and subject to impediments. Whereas that shared by human beings is without impediments, and

rational, and just, since it allots to each and every thing an equal and proportionate share of time, being, purpose, action, chance. Examine it closely. Not whether they're identical point by point, but in the aggregate: this weighed against that.

8. No time for reading. For controlling your arrogance, yes. For overcoming pain and pleasure, yes. For outgrowing ambition, yes. For not feeling anger at stupid and unpleasant people—even for caring about them—for that, yes.

9. Don't be overheard complaining about life at court. Not even to yourself.

10. Remorse is annoyance at yourself for having passed up something that's to your benefit. But if it's to your benefit it must be good—something a truly good person would be concerned about.

But no truly good person would feel remorse at passing up pleasure.

So it cannot be to your benefit, or good.

11. What is this, fundamentally? What is its nature and substance, its reason for being? What is it doing in the world? How long is it here for?

12. When you have trouble getting out of bed in the morning, remember that your defining characteristic—what defines a human being—is to work with others. Even animals know how to sleep. And it's the characteristic activity that's the more natural one—more innate and more satisfying.

13. Apply them constantly, to everything that happens: Physics. Ethics. Logic.

14. When you have to deal with someone, ask yourself: What does he mean by good and bad? If he thinks *x* or *y* about pleasure and pain (and what produces them), about fame and disgrace, about death and life, then it shouldn't shock or surprise you when he *does* *x* or *y.*

In fact, I'll remind myself that he has no real choice.

15. Remember: you shouldn't be surprised that a fig tree produces figs, nor the world what it produces. A good doctor isn't surprised when his patients have fevers, or a helmsman when the wind blows against him.

16. Remember that to change your mind and to accept correction are free acts too. The action is yours, based on your own will, your own decision—and your own mind.

17. If it's in your control, why do you do it? If it's in someone else's, then who are you blaming? Atoms? The gods? Stupid either way.

Blame no one. Set people straight, if you can. If not, just repair the damage. And suppose you can't do that either. Then where does blaming people get you?

No pointless actions.

18. What dies doesn't vanish. It stays here in the world, transformed, dissolved, as parts of the world, and of you. Which are transformed in turn—without grumbling.

19. Everything is here for a purpose, from horses to vine shoots. What's surprising about that? Even the sun will tell you, "I have a purpose," and the other gods as well. And why were *you* born? For pleasure? See if that answer will stand up to questioning.

20. Nature is like someone throwing a ball in the air, gauging its rise and arc—and where it will fall. And what does the ball gain as it flies upward? Or lose when it plummets to earth?

What does the bubble gain from its existence? Or lose by bursting?

And the same for a candle.

21. Turn it inside out: What is it like? What is it like old? Or sick? Or selling itself on the streets?

They all die soon—praiser and praised, rememberer and remembered. Remembered in these parts or in a corner of them. Even there they don't all agree with each other (or even with themselves).

And the whole earth a mere point in space.

22. Stick to what's in front of you—idea, action, utterance.

22a. This is what you deserve. You could be good today. But instead you choose tomorrow.

23. What I do? I attribute it to human beneficence.

What is done to me? I accept it—and attribute it to the gods, and that source from which all things together flow.

24. Like the baths—oil, sweat, dirt, grayish water, all of it disgusting. The whole of life, all of the visible world.

25. Verus, leaving Lucilla behind, then Lucilla. Maximus, leaving Secunda. And Secunda. Diotimus, leaving Epitynchanus. Then Epitynchanus. Faustina, leaving Antoninus. Then Antoninus.

So with all of them.

Hadrian, leaving Celer. And Celer.

Where have they gone, the brilliant, the insightful ones, the proud? Brilliant as Charax and Demetrius the Platonist and Eudaemon and the rest of them. Short-lived creatures, long dead. Some of them not remembered at all, some become legends, some lost even to legend.

So remember: your components will be scattered too, the life within you quenched. Or marching orders and another posting.

26. Joy for humans lies in human actions.

Human actions: kindness to others, contempt for the senses, the interrogation of appearances, observation of nature and of events in nature.

27. Three relationships:

   i. with the body you inhabit;
  ii. with the divine, the cause of everything in all things;
 iii. with the people around you.

28. Either pain affects the body (which is the body's problem) or it affects the soul. But the soul can choose not to be affected, preserving its own serenity, its own tranquillity. All our decisions, urges, desires, aversions lie within. No evil can touch them.

29. To erase false perceptions, tell yourself: I have it in me to keep my soul from evil, lust and all confusion. To see things as they are and treat them as they deserve. Don't overlook this innate ability.

30. To speak to the Senate—or anyone—in the right tone, without being overbearing. To choose the right words.

31. Augustus's court: his wife, his daughter, his grandsons, his step-sons, his sister, Agrippa, the relatives, servants, friends, Areius, Maecenas, the doctors, the sacrificial priests...the whole court, dead.

And consider the others...not just the deaths of individuals (like the family of the Pompeys).

That line they write on tombs—"last surviving descendant." Consider their ancestors' anxiety—that there be a successor. But someone has to be the last. There, too, the death of a whole house.

32. You have to assemble your life yourself—action by action. And be satisfied if each one achieves its goal, as far as it can. No one can keep that from happening.

—But there are external obstacles. . . .

Not to behaving with justice, self-control, and good sense.

—Well, but perhaps to some more concrete action.

But if you accept the obstacle and work with what you're given, an alternative will present itself—another piece of what you're try-ing to assemble. Action by action.

33. To accept it without arrogance, to let it go with indifference.

34. Have you ever seen a severed hand or foot, or a decapitated head, just lying somewhere far away from the body it belonged to...? That's what we do to ourselves—or try to—when we rebel against what happens to us, when we segregate ourselves. Or when we do something selfish.

You have torn yourself away from unity—your natural state, one you were born to share in. Now you've cut yourself off from it.

But you have one advantage here: you can reattach yourself. A privilege God has granted to no other part of no other whole—to be separated, cut away, and reunited. But look how he's singled us out. He's allowed us not to be broken off in the first place, and when we are he's allowed us to return, to graft ourselves back on, and take up our old position once again: part of a whole.

35. We have various abilities, present in all rational creatures as in the nature of rationality itself. And this is one of them. Just as nature takes every obstacle, every impediment, and works around it—turns it to its purposes, incorporates it into itself—so, too, a rational being can turn each setback into raw material and use it to achieve its goal.

36. Don't let your imagination be crushed by life as a whole. Don't try to picture everything bad that could possibly happen. Stick with the situation at hand, and ask, "Why is this so unbearable? Why can't I endure it?" You'll be embarrassed to answer.

Then remind yourself that past and future have no power over you. Only the present—and even that can be minimized. Just mark off its limits. And if your mind tries to claim that it can't hold out against *that*... well, then, heap shame upon it.

37. Are Pantheia or Pergamos still keeping watch at the tomb of Verus? Chabrias or Diotimus at the tomb of Hadrian? Of course they aren't. Would the emperors know it if they were?

And even if they knew, would it please them?

And even if it did, would the mourners live forever? Were they, too, not fated to grow old and then die? And when that happened, what would the emperors do?

38. The stench of decay. Rotting meat in a bag.

Look at it clearly. If you can.

39. "To the best of my judgment, when I look at the human character I see no virtue placed there to counter justice. But I see one to counter pleasure: self-control."

40. Stop perceiving the pain you imagine and you'll remain completely unaffected.

—"You?"

Your *logos.*

—But I'm not just *logos.*

Fine. Just don't let the *logos* be injured. If anything else is, let it decide that for itself.

41. For animate beings, "harmful" is whatever obstructs the operation of their senses—or the fulfillment of what they intend. Similar obstructions constitute harm to plants. So too for rational creatures, anything that obstructs the operation of the mind is harmful.

Apply this to yourself.

Do pain and pleasure have their hooks in you? Let the senses deal with it. Are there obstacles to your action? If you failed to reckon with the possibility, then that would harm you, as a rational being. But if you use common sense, you haven't been harmed or even obstructed. No one can obstruct the operations of the mind. Nothing can get at them—not fire or steel, not tyrants, not abuse—nothing. As long as it's "a sphere . . . in perfect stillness."

42. I have no right to do myself an injury. Have I ever injured anyone else if I could avoid it?

43. People find pleasure in different ways. I find it in keeping my mind clear. In not turning away from people or the things that hap-

pen to them. In accepting and welcoming everything I see. In treating each thing as it deserves.

44. Give yourself a gift: the present moment.

People out for posthumous fame forget that the Generations To Come will be the same annoying people they know now. And just as mortal. What does it matter to you if they say *x* about you, or think *y*?

45. Lift me up and hurl me. Wherever you will. My spirit will be gracious to me there—gracious and satisfied—as long as its existence and actions match its nature.

Is there any reason why my soul should suffer and be degraded—miserable, tense, huddled, frightened? How could there be?

46. What humans experience is part of human experience. The experience of the ox is part of the experience of oxen, as the vine's is of the vine, and the stone's what is proper to stones.

Nothing that can happen is unusual or unnatural, and there's no sense in complaining. Nature does not make us endure the unendurable.

47. External things are not the problem. It's your assessment of them. Which you can erase right now.

If the problem is something in your own character, who's stopping you from setting your mind straight?

And if it's that you're not doing something you think you should be, why not just do it?

—But there are insuperable obstacles.

Then it's not a problem. The cause of your inaction lies outside you.

—But how can I go on living with that undone?

Then depart, with a good conscience, as if you'd done it, embracing the obstacles too.

48. Remember that when it withdraws into itself and finds contentment there, the mind is invulnerable. It does nothing against its will, even if its resistance is irrational. And if its judgment is deliberate and grounded in logic...?

The mind without passions is a fortress. No place is more secure. Once we take refuge there we are safe forever. Not to see this is ignorance. To see it and not seek safety means misery.

49. Nothing but what you get from first impressions. That someone has insulted you, for instance. That—but not that it's done you any harm. The fact that my son is sick—that I can see. But "that he might die of it," no. Stick with first impressions. Don't extrapolate. And nothing can happen to you.

Or extrapolate. From a knowledge of all that can happen in the world.

50. The cucumber is bitter? Then throw it out.

There are brambles in the path? Then go around them.

That's all you need to know. Nothing more. Don't demand to know "why such things exist." Anyone who understands the world will laugh at you, just as a carpenter would if you seemed shocked at finding sawdust in his workshop, or a shoemaker at scraps of leather left over from work.

Of course, they have a place to dispose of these; nature has no door to sweep things out of. But the wonderful thing about its workmanship is how, faced with that limitation, it takes everything within it that seems broken, old and useless, transforms it into itself, and makes new things from it. So that it doesn't need material from any outside source, or anywhere to dispose of what's left over. It relies on itself for all it needs: space, material, and labor.

51. No carelessness in your actions. No confusion in your words. No imprecision in your thoughts. No retreating into your own soul, or trying to escape it. No overactivity.

They kill you, cut you with knives, shower you with curses. And that somehow cuts your mind off from clearness, and sanity, and self-control, and justice?

A man standing by a spring of clear, sweet water and cursing it. While the fresh water keeps on bubbling up. He can shovel mud into it, or dung, and the stream will carry it away, wash itself clean, remain unstained.

To have that. Not a cistern but a perpetual spring.

How? By working to win your freedom. Hour by hour. Through patience, honesty, humility.

52. Not to know what the world is is to be ignorant of where you are.

Not to know why it's here is to be ignorant of who you are. And what it is.

Not to know any of this is to be ignorant of why *you're* here.

And what are we to make of anyone who cares about the applause of such people, who don't know where or who they are?

53. You want praise from people who kick themselves every fifteen minutes, the approval of people who despise themselves. (Is it a sign of self-respect to regret nearly everything you do?)

54. To join ourselves not just to the air surrounding us, through breath, but to the reason that embraces all things, through thought.

Reason is just as omnipresent, just as widely diffused in those who accept it as air is in those who breathe.

55. The existence of evil does not harm the world. And an individual act of evil does not harm the victim. Only one person is harmed by it—and he can stop being harmed as soon as he decides to.

56. Other people's wills are as independent of mine as their breath and bodies. We may exist for the sake of one another, but our will rules its own domain. Otherwise the harm they do would cause harm to me. Which is not what God intended—for my happiness to rest with someone else.

57. We speak of the sun's light as "pouring down on us," as "pouring over us" in all directions. Yet it's never poured out. Because it doesn't really pour; it extends. Its beams (*aktai*) get their name from their extension (*ekteinesthai*).

To see the nature of a sunbeam, look at light as it falls through a narrow opening into a dark room. It extends in a straight line, striking any solid object that stands in its way and blocks the space beyond it. There it remains—not vanishing, or falling away.

That's what the outpouring—the diffusion—of thought should be like: not emptied out, but extended. And not striking at obstacles with fury and violence, or falling away before them, but holding its ground and illuminating what receives it.

What doesn't transmit light creates its own darkness.

58. Fear of death is fear of what we may experience. Nothing at all, or something quite new. But if we experience nothing, we can experience nothing bad. And if our experience changes, then our existence will change with it—change, but not cease.

59. People exist for one another. You can instruct or endure them.

60. An arrow has one motion and the mind another. Even when pausing, even when weighing conclusions, the mind is moving forward, toward its goal.

61. To enter others' minds and let them enter yours.

BOOK 9

1. Injustice is a kind of blasphemy. Nature designed rational beings for each other's sake: to help—not harm—one another, as they deserve. To transgress its will, then, is to blaspheme against the oldest of the gods.

And to lie is to blaspheme against it too. Because "nature" means the nature of that which is. And that which is and that which is the case are closely linked, so that nature is synonymous with Truth—the source of all true things. To lie deliberately is to blaspheme—the liar commits deceit, and thus injustice. And likewise to lie without realizing it. Because the involuntary liar disrupts the harmony of nature—its order. He is in conflict with the way the world is structured. As anyone is who deviates toward what is opposed to the truth—even against his will. Nature gave him the resources to distinguish between true and false. And he neglected them, and now can't tell the difference.

And to pursue pleasure as good, and flee from pain as evil—that too is blasphemous. Someone who does that is bound to find himself constantly reproaching nature—complaining that it doesn't treat the good and bad as they deserve, but often lets the bad enjoy pleasure and the things that produce it, and makes the good suffer pain, and the things that produce pain. And moreover, to fear pain is to fear something that's bound to happen, the world being what it is—and that again is blasphemy. While if you pursue pleasure, you can hardly avoid wrongdoing—which is manifestly blasphemous.

Some things nature is indifferent to; if it privileged one over the other it would hardly have created both. And if we want to follow nature, to be of one mind with it, we need to share its indifference. To privilege pleasure over pain—life over death, fame over anonymity—is clearly blasphemous. Nature certainly doesn't.

And when I say that nature is indifferent to them, I mean that they happen indifferently, at different times, to the things that exist and the things that come into being after them, through some ancient decree of Providence—the decree by which from some initial starting point it embarked on the creation that we know, by laying down the principles of what was to come and determining the generative forces: existence and change, and their successive stages.

2. Real good luck would be to abandon life without ever encountering dishonesty, or hypocrisy, or self-indulgence, or pride. But the "next best voyage" is to die when you've had enough. Or are you determined to lie down with evil? Hasn't experience even taught you *that*—to avoid it like the plague? Because it *is* a plague—a mental cancer—worse than anything caused by tainted air or an unhealthy climate. Diseases like that can only threaten your life; this one attacks your humanity.

3. Don't look down on death, but welcome it. It too is one of the things required by nature. Like youth and old age. Like growth and maturity. Like a new set of teeth, a beard, the first gray hair. Like sex and pregnancy and childbirth. Like all the other physical changes at each stage of life, our dissolution is no different.

So this is how a thoughtful person should await death: not with indifference, not with impatience, not with disdain, but simply viewing it as one of the things that happen to us. Now you anticipate the child's emergence from its mother's womb; that's how you should await the hour when your soul will emerge from its compartment.

Or perhaps you need some tidy aphorism to tuck away in the back of your mind. Well, consider two things that should reconcile you to death: the nature of the things you'll leave behind you, and the kind of people you'll no longer be mixed up with. There's no need to feel resentment toward them—in fact, you should look out for their well-being, and be gentle with them—but keep in mind that everything you believe is meaningless to those you leave behind. Because that's all that could restrain us (if anything could)—the only thing that could make us want to stay here: the chance to live with those who share our vision. But now? Look how tiring it is—this cacophony we live in. Enough to make you say to death, "Come quickly. Before I start to forget myself, like them."

4. To do harm is to do yourself harm. To do an injustice is to do yourself an injustice—it degrades you.

5. And you can also commit injustice by doing nothing.

6. Objective judgment, now, at this very moment.
   Unselfish action, now, at this very moment.
   Willing acceptance—now, at this very moment—of all
      external events.
   That's all you need.

7. Blot out your imagination. Turn your desire to stone. Quench your appetites. Keep your mind centered on itself.

8. Animals without the *logos* are assigned the same soul, and those who have the *logos* share one too—a rational one. Just as all earthly creatures share one earth. Just as we all see by the same light, and breathe the same air—all of us who see and breathe.

9. All things are drawn toward what is like them, if such a thing exists. All earthly things feel the earth's tug. All wet things flow together. And airy things as well, so they have to be forcibly prevented from mixing. Fire is naturally drawn upward by that higher fire, but ready to ignite at the slightest touch of other, earthly flame. So that anything drier than usual makes good fuel, because less of what hinders combustion is mixed in with it.

And things that share an intelligent nature are just as prone to seek out what is like them. If not more so. Because their superiority in other ways is matched by their greater readiness to mix and mingle with their counterparts.

Even in irrational beings we see swarms and herds, and nesting, and love not unlike ours. Because they do have souls, and the bonding instinct is found in a developed form—not something we see in plants, or stones, or trees. And it's still more developed in rational beings, with their states, friendships, families, groups, their treaties and truces. And in those yet more developed there is a kind of unity even between separate things, the kind that we see in the stars. An advanced level of development can produce a sympathy even in things that are quite distinct.

But look how things are now. The rational things are the only ones that have lost that sense of attraction—of convergence. Only there do we not see that intermingling. But however much they try to avoid it, there's no escaping. Nature is stronger. As you can see if you look closely.

Concrete objects can pull free of the earth more easily than humans can escape humanity.

10. Humanity, divinity, and the world: all of them bearing fruit. Each fruitful in its season. Normally we limit the word to vines and other plants. Unnecessarily. The fruit of the *logos* nourishes both us

and it. And other things spring from it too—of the same species as the *logos* itself.

11. Convince them not to.

If you can.

And if not, remember: the capacity for patience was given us for a reason. The gods are patient with them too, and even help them to concrete things: health, money, fame. ... Such is the gods' goodness.

And yours, too, if you wanted. What's stopping you?

12. Work:

Not to rouse pity, not to win sympathy or admiration. Only this: Activity.

Stillness.

As the *logos* of the state requires.

13. Today I escaped from anxiety. Or no, I discarded it, because it was within me, in my own perceptions—not outside.

14. Known by long experience, limited in life span, debased in substance—all of it.

Now as then, in the time of those we buried.

15. Things wait outside us, hover at the door. They keep to themselves. Ask them who they are and they don't know, they can give no account of themselves.

What accounts for them?

The mind does.

16. Not being done to, but doing—the source of good and bad for rational and political beings. Where their own goodness and badness is found—not in being done to, but in doing.

17. A rock thrown in the air. It loses nothing by coming down, gained nothing by going up.

18. Enter their minds, and you'll find the judges you're so afraid of—and how judiciously they judge themselves.

19. Everything in flux. And you too will alter in the whirl and perish, and the world as well.

20. Leave other people's mistakes where they lie.

21. When we cease from activity, or follow a thought to its conclusion, it's a kind of death. And it doesn't harm us. Think about your life: childhood, boyhood, youth, old age. Every transformation a kind of dying. Was that so terrible?

Think about life with your grandfather, your mother, your adopted father. Realize how many other deaths and transformations and endings there have been and ask yourself: Was that so terrible?

Then neither will the close of your life be—its ending and transformation.

22. Go straight to the seat of intelligence—your own, the world's, your neighbor's.

Your own—to ground it in justice.

The world's—to remind yourself what it is that you're part of.

Your neighbor's—to distinguish ignorance from calculation. And recognize it as like yours.

23. You participate in a society by your existence. Then participate in its life through your actions—all your actions. Any action not directed toward a social end (directly or indirectly) is a disturbance to your life, an obstacle to wholeness, a source of dissension. Like the man in the Assembly—a faction to himself, always out of step with the majority.

24. Childish tantrums, children's games, "spirits carrying corpses"; "Odysseus in the Underworld" saw more real life.

25. Identify its purpose—what makes it what it is—and examine that. (Ignore its concrete form.) Then calculate the length of time that such a thing was meant to last.

26. Endless suffering—all from not allowing the mind to do its job. Enough.

27. When you face someone's insults, hatred, whatever . . . look at his soul. Get inside him. Look at what sort of person he is. You'll find you don't need to strain to impress him.

But you do have to wish him well. He's your closest relative. The gods assist him just as they do you—by signs and dreams and every other way—to get the things he wants.

28. The world's cycles never change—up and down, from age to age.

Either the world's intelligence wills each thing (if so, accept its will), or it exercised that will once—once and for all—and all else follows as a consequence (and if so, why worry?).

One way or another: atoms or unity. If it's God, all is well. If it's arbitrary, don't imitate it.

The earth will cover us all, and then be transformed in turn, and that too will change, ad infinitum. And that as well, ad infinitum.

Think about them: the waves of change and alteration, endlessly breaking. And see our brief mortality for what it is.

29. The design of the world is like a flood, sweeping all before it. The foolishness of them—little men busy with affairs of state, with philosophy—or what they think of as philosophy. Nothing but phlegm and mucus.

—Well, then what?

Do what nature demands. Get a move on—if you have it in you—and don't worry whether anyone will give you credit for it. And don't go expecting Plato's Republic; be satisfied with even the smallest progress, and treat the outcome of it all as unimportant.

Who can change their minds? And without that change, what is there but groaning, slavery, a pretense of obedience? Go on and cite Alexander, Philip, Demetrius of Phalerum. Whether they knew nature's will and made themselves its student is for them to say. And if they preferred to play the king? Well, no one forced me to be their understudy.

The task of philosophy is modest and straightforward. Don't tempt me to presumption.

30. To see them from above: the thousands of animal herds, the rituals, the voyages on calm or stormy seas, the different ways we come into the world, share it with one another, and leave it. Consider the lives led once by others, long ago, the lives to be led by others after you, the lives led even now, in foreign lands. How many people don't even know your name. How many will soon have forgotten it. How many offer you praise now—and tomorrow, perhaps, contempt.

That to be remembered is worthless. Like fame. Like everything.

31. Indifference to external events.

And a commitment to justice in your own acts.

Which means: thought and action resulting in the common good.

What you were born to do.

32. You can discard most of the junk that clutters your mind—things that exist only there—and clear out space for yourself:

>   …by comprehending the scale of the world
>   …by contemplating infinite time
>   …by thinking of the speed with which things change—each part of every thing; the narrow space between our birth and death; the infinite time before; the equally unbounded time that follows.

33. All that you see will soon have vanished, and those who see it vanish will vanish themselves, and the ones who reached old age have no advantage over the untimely dead.

34. What their minds are like. What they work at. What evokes their love and admiration.

Imagine their souls stripped bare. And their vanity. To suppose that their disdain could harm anyone—or their praise help them.

35. To decompose is to be recomposed.

That's what nature does. Nature—through whom all things happen as they should, and have happened forever in just the same way, and will continue to, one way or another, endlessly.

That things happen for the worst and always will, that the gods have no power to regulate them, and the world is condemned to never-ending evil—how can you say that?

36. Disgust at what things are made of: Liquid, dust, bones, filth. Or marble as hardened dirt, gold and silver as residues, clothes as hair, purple dye as shellfish blood. And all the rest.

And the same with our living breath—transformed from one thing to another.

37. Enough of this wretched, whining monkey life.

What's the matter? Is any of this new? What is it you find surprising?

The purpose? Look at it.

The material? Look at that.

That's all there is.

And the gods? Well, you could try being simpler, gentler. Even now.

A hundred years or three.... No difference.

38. If they've injured you, then they're the ones who suffer for it.

But have they?

39. Either all things spring from one intelligent source and form a single body (and the part should accept the actions of the whole) or there are only atoms, joining and splitting forever, and nothing else.

So why feel anxiety?

Say to your mind: Are you dead? damaged? brutal? dishonest?

Are you one of the herd? or grazing like one?

40. Either the gods have power or they don't. If they don't, why pray? If they do, then why not pray for something else instead of for things to happen or not to happen? Pray not to feel fear. Or desire, or grief. If the gods can do anything, they can surely do that for us.

—But those are things the gods left up to me.

Then isn't it better to do what's up to you—like a free man—than to be passively controlled by what isn't, like a slave or beggar? And what makes you think the gods don't care about what's up to us?

Start praying like this and you'll see.

Not "some way to sleep with her"—but a way to stop wanting to.

Not "some way to get rid of him"—but a way to stop trying.

Not "some way to save my child"—but a way to lose your fear.

Redirect your prayers like that, and watch what happens.

41. Epicurus: "During my illness, my conversations were not about my physical state; I did not waste my visitors' time with things of that sort, but went on discussing philosophy, and concentrated on one point in particular: how the mind can participate in the sensations of the body and yet maintain its serenity, and focus on its own well-being. Nor did I let my doctors strut about like grandees. I went on living my life the way it should be lived."

Like that. In illness—or any other situation.

Not to let go of philosophy, no matter what happens; not to bandy words with crackpots and philistines—good rules for any philosopher.

Concentrate on what you're doing, and what you're doing it with.

42. When you run up against someone else's shamelessness, ask yourself this: Is a world without shamelessness possible?

No.

Then don't ask the impossible. There have to be shameless people in the world. This is one of them.

The same for someone vicious or untrustworthy, or with any other defect. Remembering that the whole class has to exist will make you more tolerant of its members.

Another useful point to bear in mind: What qualities has nature given us to counter that defect? As an antidote to unkindness it gave us kindness. And other qualities to balance other flaws.

And when others stray off course, you can always try to set them straight, because every wrongdoer is doing something wrong—doing something *the wrong way*.

And how does it injure you anyway? You'll find that none of the people you're upset about has done anything that could do damage to your mind. But that's all that "harm" or "injury" could mean. Yes, boorish people do boorish things. What's strange or unheard-of about that? Isn't it yourself you should reproach—for not anticipating that they'd act this way? The *logos* gave you the means to see it—that a given person would act a given way—but you paid no attention. And now you're astonished that he's gone and done it. So when you call someone "untrustworthy" or "ungrateful," turn the reproach on yourself. It was *you* who did wrong. By assuming that someone with those traits deserved your trust. Or by doing them a favor and expecting something in return, instead of looking to the action itself for your reward. What else did you expect from helping someone out? Isn't it enough that you've done what your nature demands? You want a salary for it too? As if your eyes expected a reward for seeing, or your feet for walking. That's what they were made for. By doing what they were designed to do, they're performing their function. Whereas humans were made to help others. And when we do help others—or help them to do something—we're doing what we were designed for. We perform our function.

BOOK 10

1. To my soul:

Are you ever going to achieve goodness? Ever going to be simple, whole, and naked—as plain to see as the body that contains you? Know what an affectionate and loving disposition would feel like? Ever be fulfilled, ever stop desiring—lusting and longing for people and things to enjoy? Or for more time to enjoy them? Or for some other place or country—"a more temperate clime"? Or for people easier to get along with? And instead be satisfied with what you have, and accept the present—all of it. And convince yourself that everything is the gift of the gods, that things are good and always will be, whatever they decide and have in store for the preservation of that perfect entity—good and just and beautiful, creating all things, connecting and embracing them, and gathering in their separated fragments to create more like them.

Will you ever take your stand as a fellow citizen with gods and human beings, blaming no one, deserving no one's censure?

2. Focus on what nature demands, as if you were governed by that alone. Then do that, and accept it, unless your nature as a living being would be degraded by it.

Then focus on what *that* nature demands, and accept that too—unless your nature as a rational being would be degraded by it.

And, of course, "rational" also implies "civic."

Follow these guidelines and don't waste time on anything else.

3. Everything that happens is either endurable or not.

If it's endurable, then endure it. Stop complaining.

If it's unendurable... then stop complaining. Your destruction will mean its end as well.

Just remember: you can endure anything your mind can make endurable, by treating it as in your interest to do so.

In your interest, or in your nature.

4. If they've made a mistake, correct them gently and show them where they went wrong. If you can't do that, then the blame lies with you. Or no one.

5. Whatever happens to you has been waiting to happen since the beginning of time. The twining strands of fate wove both of them together: your own existence and the things that happen to you.

6. Whether it's atoms or nature, the first thing to be said is this: I am a part of a world controlled by nature. Secondly: that I have a relationship with other, similar parts. And with that in mind I have no right, as a part, to complain about what is assigned me by the whole. Because what benefits the whole can't harm the parts, and the whole does nothing that doesn't benefit it. That's a trait shared by all natures, but the nature of the world is defined by a second characteristic as well: no outside force can compel it to cause itself harm.

So by keeping in mind the whole I form a part of, I'll accept whatever happens. And because of my relationship to other parts, I will do nothing selfish, but aim instead to join them, to direct my every action toward what benefits us all and to avoid what doesn't. If I do all that, then my life should go smoothly. As you might expect a citizen's life to go—one whose actions serve his fellow citizens, and who embraces the community's decree.

7. The whole is compounded by nature of individual parts, whose destruction is inevitable ("destruction" here meaning transformation). If the process is harmful to the parts and unavoidable, then it's hard to see how the whole can run smoothly, with parts of it passing from one state to another, all of them built only to be destroyed in different ways. Does nature set out to cause its own components harm, and make them vulnerable to it—indeed, predestined to it? Or is it oblivious to what goes on? Neither one seems very plausible.

But suppose we throw out "nature" and explain these things through inherent properties. It would still be absurd to say that the individual things in the world are inherently prone to change, and at the same time be astonished at it or complain—on the grounds that it was happening "contrary to nature." And least of all when things return to the state from which they came. Because our elements are either simply dispersed, or are subject to a kind of gravitation—the solid portions being pulled toward earth, and what is ethereal drawn into the air, until they're absorbed into the universal *logos*—which is subject to periodic conflagrations, or renewed through continual change.

And don't imagine either that those elements—the solid ones and the ethereal—are with us from our birth. Their influx took place yesterday, or the day before—from the food we ate, the air we breathed.

And that's what changes—not the person your mother gave birth to.

—But if you're inextricably linked to it through your sense of individuality?

That's not what we're talking about here.

8. Epithets for yourself: Upright. Modest. Straightforward. Sane. Cooperative. Disinterested.

Try not to exchange them for others.

And if you should forfeit them, set about getting them back.

Keep in mind that "sanity" means understanding things—each individual thing—for what they are. And not losing the thread.

And "cooperation" means accepting what nature assigns you—accepting it willingly.

And "disinterest" means that the intelligence should rise above the movements of the flesh—the rough and the smooth alike. Should rise above fame, above death, and everything like them.

If you maintain your claim to these epithets—without caring if others apply them to you or not—you'll become a new person, living a new life. To keep on being the person that you've been—to keep being mauled and degraded by the life you're living—is to be devoid of sense and much too fond of life. Like those animal fighters at the games—torn half to pieces, covered in blood and gore, and still pleading to be held over till tomorrow...to be bitten and clawed again.

Set sail, then, with this handful of epithets to guide you. And steer a steady course, if you can. Like an emigrant to the islands of the blest. And if you feel yourself adrift—as if you've lost control—then hope for the best, and put in somewhere where you can regain it. Or leave life altogether, not in anger, but matter-of-factly, straightforwardly, without arrogance, in the knowledge that you've at least done that much with your life.

And as you try to keep these epithets in mind, it will help you a great deal to keep the gods in mind as well. What they want is not flattery, but for rational things to be like them. For figs to do what figs were meant to do—and dogs, and bees... and people.

9. Operatics, combat and confusion. Sloth and servility. Every day they blot out those sacred principles of yours—which you daydream thoughtlessly about, or just let slide.

Your actions and perceptions need to aim:

• at accomplishing practical ends
• at the exercise of thought
• at maintaining a confidence founded on understanding. An unobtrusive confidence—hidden in plain sight.

When will you let yourself enjoy straightforwardness? Seriousness? Or understanding individual things—their nature and substance, their place in the world, their life span, their composition, who can possess them, whose they are to give and to receive?

10. Spiders are proud of catching flies, men of catching hares, fish in a net, boars, bears, Sarmatians...

Criminal psychology.

11. How they all change into one another—acquire the ability to see that. Apply it constantly; use it to train yourself. Nothing is as conducive to spiritual growth.

11a. He has stripped away his body and—realizing that at some point soon he will have to abandon mankind and leave all this behind—has dedicated himself to serving justice in all he does, and nature in all that happens. What people say or think about him, or how they treat him, isn't something he worries about. Only these two questions: Is what he's doing now the right thing to be doing? Does he accept and welcome what he's been assigned? He has stripped away all other occupations, all other tasks. He wants only to travel a straight path—to God, by way of law.

12. Why all this guesswork? You can see what needs to be done. If you can see the road, follow it. Cheerfully, without turning back. If not, hold up and get the best advice you can. If anything gets in the way, forge on ahead, making good use of what you have on hand, sticking to what seems right. (The best goal to achieve, and the one we fall short of when we fail.)

12a. To follow the *logos* in all things is to be relaxed and energetic, joyful and serious at once.

13. When you wake up, ask yourself:
Does it make any difference to you if other people blame you for doing what's right?
It makes no difference.
Have you forgotten what the people who are so vociferous in praise or blame of others are like as they sleep and eat? Forgotten their behavior, their fears, their desires, their thefts and depredations—not physical ones, but those committed by what should be highest in them? What creates, when it chooses, loyalty, humility, truth, order, well-being.

14. Nature gives and nature takes away. Anyone with sense and humility will tell her, "Give and take as you please," not out of defiance, but out of obedience and goodwill.

15. Only a short time left. Live as if you were alone—out in the wilderness. No difference between here and there: the city that you live in is the world.
Let people see someone living naturally, and understand what

that means. Let them kill him if they can't stand it. (Better than living like this.)

16. To stop talking about what the good man is like, and just be one.

17. Continual awareness of all time and space, of the size and life span of the things around us. A grape seed in infinite space. A half twist of a corkscrew against eternity.

18. Bear in mind that everything that exists is already fraying at the edges, and in transition, subject to fragmentation and to rot.
   Or that everything was born to die.

19. How they act when they eat and sleep and mate and defecate and all the rest. Then when they order and exult, or rage and thunder from on high. And yet, just consider the things they submitted to a moment ago, and the reasons for it—and the things they'll submit to again before very long.

20. Each of us needs what nature gives us, when nature gives it.

21. "The earth knows longing for the rain, the sky/knows longing..." And the world longs to create what will come to be. I tell it "I share your longing."
   (And isn't that what we mean by "inclined to happen"?)

22. Possibilities:

   i. To keep on living (you should be used to it by now)
   ii. To end it (it was your choice, after all)
   iii. To die (having met your obligations)

   Those are the only options. Reason for optimism.

23. Keep always before you that "this is no different from an empty field," and the things in it are the same as on a mountaintop, on the seashore, wherever. Plato gets to the heart of it: "fencing a sheepfold in the mountains, and milking goats or sheep."

24. My mind. What is it? What am I making of it? What am I using it for?

Is it empty of thought?

Isolated and torn loose from those around it?

Melted into flesh and blended with it, so that it shares its urges?

25. When a slave runs away from his master, we call him a fugitive slave. But the law of nature is a master too, and to break it is to become a fugitive.

To feel grief, anger or fear is to try to escape from something decreed by the ruler of all things, now or in the past or in the future. And that ruler is law, which governs what happens to each of us. To feel grief or anger or fear is to become a fugitive—a fugitive from justice.

26. He deposits his sperm and leaves. And then a force not his takes it and goes to work, and creates a child.

This ... from *that?*

Or:

He pours food down his throat. And then a force not his takes it and creates sensations, desires, daily life, physical strength and so much else besides.

To look at these things going on silently and see the force that drives them. As we see the force that pushes things and pulls them. Not with our eyes, but just as clearly.

27. To bear in mind constantly that all of this has happened before. And will happen again—the same plot from beginning to end, the identical staging. Produce them in your mind, as you know them from experience or from history: the court of Hadrian, of Antoninus. The courts of Philip, Alexander, Croesus. All just the same. Only the people different.

28. People who feel hurt and resentment: picture them as the pig at the sacrifice, kicking and squealing all the way.

Like the man alone in his bed, silently weeping over the chains that bind us.

That everything has to submit. But only rational beings can do so voluntarily.

29. Stop whatever you're doing for a moment and ask yourself: Am I afraid of death because I won't be able to do *this* anymore?

30. When faced with people's bad behavior, turn around and ask when *you* have acted like that. When you saw money as a good, or pleasure, or social position. Your anger will subside as soon as you recognize that they acted under compulsion (what else could they do?).

Or remove the compulsion, if you can.

31. When you look at Satyron, see Socraticus, or Eutyches, or Hymen.

When you look at Euphrates, see Eutychion or Silvanus.

With Alciphron, see Tropaeophorus.

When you look at Xenophon, see Crito or Severus.

When you look at yourself, see any of the emperors.

And the same with everyone else. Then let it hit you: Where are they now?

Nowhere . . . or wherever.

That way you'll see human life for what it is. Smoke. Nothing. Especially when you recall that once things alter they cease to exist through all the endless years to come.

Then why such turmoil? To live your brief life rightly, isn't that enough?

The raw material you're missing, the opportunities . . . ! What is any of this but training—training for your *logos*, in life observed accurately, scientifically.

So keep at it, until it's fully digested. As a strong stomach digests whatever it eats. As a blazing fire takes whatever you throw on it, and makes it light and flame.

32. That no one can say truthfully that you are not a straightforward or honest person. That anyone who thinks that believes a falsehood. The responsibility is all yours; no one can stop you from being honest or straightforward. Simply resolve not to go on living if you aren't. It would be contrary to the *logos*.

33. Given the material we're made of, what's the sanest thing that we can do or say? Whatever it may be, you can do or say it. Don't pretend that anything's stopping you.

You'll never stop complaining until you feel the same pleasure that the hedonist gets from self-indulgence—only from doing what's proper to human beings as far as circumstances—inherent or fortuitous—allow. "Enjoyment" means doing as much of what your nature requires as you can. And you can do that anywhere. A privilege not granted to a cylinder—to determine its own action. Or to water, or fire, or any of the other things governed by nature alone, or by an irrational soul. Too many things obstruct them and get in their way. But the intellect and *logos* are able to make their way through anything in their path—by inborn capacity or sheer force of will. Keep before your eyes the ease with which they do this—the ease with which the *logos* is carried through all things, as fire is drawn upward or a stone falls to earth, as a cylinder rolls down an inclined plane.

That's all you need. All other obstacles either affect the lifeless body, or have no power to shake or harm anything unless misperception takes over or the *logos* surrenders voluntarily. Otherwise those they obstruct would be degraded by them immediately. In all other entities, when anything bad happens to them, it affects them for the worse. Whereas here a person is improved by it (if I can put it like that)—and we admire him for reacting as a person should.

And keep in mind that nothing can harm one of nature's citizens except what harms the city he belongs to. And nothing harms that city except what harms its law. And there is no so-called misfortune that can do that. So long as the law is safe, so is the city—and the citizen.

34. If you've immersed yourself in the principles of truth, the briefest, most random reminder is enough to dispel all fear and pain:

> …leaves that the wind
> Drives earthward; such are the generations of men.

Your children, leaves.
Leaves applauding loyally and heaping praise upon you, or turning around and calling down curses, sneering and mocking from a safe distance.
A glorious reputation handed down by leaves.

All of these "spring up in springtime"—and the wind blows them all away. And the tree puts forth others to replace them.

None of us have much time. And yet you act as if things were eternal—the way you fear and long for them. . . .

Before long, darkness. And whoever buries you mourned in their turn.

35. A healthy pair of eyes should see everything that can be seen and not say, "No! Too bright!" (which is a symptom of ophthalmia).

A healthy sense of hearing or smell should be prepared for any sound or scent; a healthy stomach should have the same reaction to all foods, as a mill to what it grinds.

So too a healthy mind should be prepared for anything. The one that keeps saying, "Are my children all right?" or "Everyone must approve of me" is like eyes that can only stand pale colors, or teeth that can handle only mush.

36. It doesn't matter how good a life you've led. There'll still be people standing around the bed who will welcome the sad event.

Even with the intelligent and good. Won't there be someone thinking "Finally! To be through with that old schoolteacher. Even though he never said anything, you could always *feel* him judging you." And that's for a good man. How many traits do *you* have that would make a lot of people glad to be rid of you?

Remember that, when the time comes. You'll be less reluctant to leave if you can tell yourself, "This is the sort of life I'm leaving. Even the people around me, the ones I spent so much time fighting for, praying over, caring about—even they want me gone, in hopes that it will make their own lives easier. How could anyone stand a longer stay here?"

And yet, don't leave angry with them. Be true to who you are: caring, sympathetic, kind. And not as if you were being torn away from life. But the way it is when someone dies peacefully, how the soul is released from the body—that's how you should leave them. It was nature that bound you to them—that tied the knot. And nature that now unties you.

I am released from those around me. Not dragged against my will, but unresisting.

There are things that nature demands. And this is one of them.

37. Learn to ask of all actions, "Why are they doing that?"
    Starting with your own.

38. Remember that what pulls the strings is within—hidden from us. Is speech, is life, is the person. Don't conceive of the rest as part of it—the skin that contains it, and the accompanying organs. Which are tools—like a carpenter's axe, except that they're attached to us from birth, and are no more use without what moves and holds them still than the weaver's shuttle, the writer's pencil, the driver's whip.

BOOK 11

1. Characteristics of the rational soul:

Self-perception, self-examination, and the power to make of itself whatever it wants.

It reaps its own harvest, unlike plants (and, in a different way, animals), whose yield is gathered in by others.

It reaches its intended goal, no matter where the limit of its life is set. Not like dancing and theater and things like that, where the performance is incomplete if it's broken off in the middle, but at any point—no matter which one you pick—it has fulfilled its mission, done its work completely. So that it can say, "I have what I came for."

It surveys the world and the empty space around it, and the way it's put together. It delves into the endlessness of time to extend its grasp and comprehension of the periodic births and rebirths that the world goes through. It knows that those who come after us will see nothing different, that those who came before us saw no more than we do, and that anyone with forty years behind him and eyes in his head has seen both past and future—both alike.

Also characteristic of the rational soul:

Affection for its neighbors. Truthfulness. Humility. Not to place anything above itself—which is characteristic of law as well. No difference here between the *logos* of rationality and that of justice.

2. To acquire indifference to pretty singing, to dancing, to the martial arts: Analyze the melody into the notes that form it, and as you hear each one, ask yourself whether you're powerless against *that*. That should be enough to deter you.

The same with dancing: individual movements and tableaux. And the same with the martial arts.

And with everything—except virtue and what springs from it. Look at the individual parts and move from analysis to indifference.

Apply this to life as a whole.

3. The resolute soul:

Resolute in separation from the body. And then in dissolution or fragmentation—or continuity.

But the resolution has to be the result of its own decision, not just in response to outside forces [like the Christians]. It has to be considered and serious, persuasive to other people. Without dramatics.

4. Have I done something for the common good? Then I share in the benefits.

To stay centered on that. Not to give up.

5. "And your profession?" "Goodness." (And how is that to be achieved, except by thought—about the world, about the nature of people?)

6. First, tragedies. To remind us of what can happen, and that it happens inevitably—and if something gives you pleasure on *that* stage, it shouldn't cause you anger on this one. You realize that these are things we all have to go through, and that even those who

cry aloud "o Mount Cithaeron!" have to endure them. And some
excellent lines as well. These, for example:

> If I and my two children cannot move the gods
> The gods must have their reasons

Or:

> And why should we feel anger at the world?

And:

> To harvest life like standing stalks of grain

and a good many others.

Then, after tragedy, Old Comedy: instructive in its frankness,
its plain speaking designed to puncture pretensions. (Diogenes
used the same tactic for similar ends.)

Then consider the Middle (and later the New) Comedy and
what it aimed at—gradually degenerating into mere realism and
empty technique. There are undeniably good passages, even in
those writers, but what was the point of it all—the script and staging alike?

7. It stares you in the face. No role is so well suited to philosophy
as the one you happen to be in right now.

8. A branch cut away from the branch beside it is simultaneously
cut away from the whole tree. So too a human being separated from
another is cut loose from the whole community.

The branch is cut off by someone else. But people cut themselves off—through hatred, through rejection—and don't realize
that they're cutting themselves off from the whole civic enterprise.

Except that we also have a gift, given us by Zeus, who founded this community of ours. We can reattach ourselves and become once more components of the whole.

But if the rupture is too often repeated, it makes the severed part hard to reconnect, and to restore. You can see the difference between the branch that's been there since the beginning, remaining on the tree and growing with it, and the one that's been cut off and grafted back.

"One trunk, two minds." As the gardeners put it.

9. As you move forward in the *logos*, people will stand in your way. They can't keep you from doing what's healthy; don't let them stop you from putting up with them either. Take care on both counts. Not just sound judgments, solid actions—tolerance as well, for those who try to obstruct us or give us trouble in other ways.

Because anger, too, is weakness, as much as breaking down and giving up the struggle. Both are deserters: the man who breaks and runs, and the one who lets himself be alienated from his fellow humans.

10. The natural can never be inferior to the artificial; art imitates nature, not the reverse. In which case, that most highly developed and comprehensive nature—Nature itself—cannot fall short of artifice in its craftsmanship.

Now, all the arts move from lower goals to higher ones. Won't Nature do the same?

Hence justice. Which is the source of all the other virtues. For how could we do what justice requires if we are distracted by things that don't matter, if we are naive, gullible, inconstant?

11. It's the pursuit of these things, and your attempts to avoid them, that leave you in such turmoil. And yet they aren't seeking you out; you are the one seeking them.

Suspend judgment about them. And at once they will lie still, and you will be freed from fleeing and pursuing.

12. The soul as a sphere in equilibrium: Not grasping at things beyond it or retreating inward. Not fragmenting outward, not sinking back on itself, but ablaze with light and looking at the truth, without and within.

13. Someone despises me.

That's their problem.

Mine: not to do or say anything despicable.

Someone hates me. Their problem.

Mine: to be patient and cheerful with everyone, including them. Ready to show them their mistake. Not spitefully, or to show off my own self-control, but in an honest, upright way. Like Phocion (if he wasn't just pretending). That's what we should be like inside, and never let the gods catch us feeling anger or resentment.

As long as you do what's proper to your nature, and accept what the world's nature has in store—as long as you work for others' good, by any and all means—what is there that can harm you?

14. They flatter one another out of contempt, and their desire to rule one another makes them bow and scrape.

15. The despicable phoniness of people who say, "Listen, I'm going to level with you here." What does that mean? It shouldn't even need to be said. It should be obvious—written in block letters on your forehead. It should be audible in your voice, visible in your eyes, like a lover who looks into your face and takes in the whole story at a glance. A straightforward, honest person should be like someone who stinks: when you're in the same room with him, you know it. But false straightforwardness is like a knife in the back.

False friendship is the worst. Avoid it at all costs. If you're honest and straightforward and mean well, it should show in your eyes. It should be unmistakable.

16. To live a good life:

We have the potential for it. If we can learn to be indifferent to what makes no difference. This is how we learn: by looking at each thing, both the parts and the whole. Keeping in mind that none of them can dictate how we perceive it. They don't impose themselves on us. They hover before us, unmoving. It is we who generate the judgments—inscribing them on ourselves. And we don't have to. We could leave the page blank—and if a mark slips through, erase it instantly.

Remember how brief is the attentiveness required. And then our lives will end.

And why is it so hard when things go against you? If it's imposed by nature, accept it gladly and stop fighting it. And if not, work out what your own nature requires, and aim at that, even if it brings you no glory.

None of us is forbidden to pursue our own good.

17. Source and substance of each thing. What it changes into, and what it's like transformed; that nothing can harm it.

18.   i. My relationship to them. That we came into the world for the sake of one another. Or from another point of view, I came into it to be their guardian—as the ram is of the flock, and the bull of the herd.

Start from this: if not atoms, then Nature—directing everything. In that case, lower things for the sake of higher ones, and higher ones for one another.

ii. What they're like eating, in bed, etc. How driven they are by their beliefs. How proud they are of what they do.

iii. That if they're right to do this, then you have no right to complain. And if they aren't, then they do it involuntarily, out of ignorance. Because all souls are prevented from treating others as they deserve, just as they are kept from truth: unwillingly. Which is why they resent being called unjust, or arrogant, or greedy—any suggestion that they aren't good neighbors.

iv. That you've made enough mistakes yourself. You're just like them.

Even if there are some you've avoided, you have the potential.

Even if cowardice has kept you from them. Or fear of what people would say. Or some equally bad reason.

v. That you don't know for sure it *is* a mistake. A lot of things are means to some other end. You have to know an awful lot before you can judge other people's actions with real understanding.

vi. When you lose your temper, or even feel irritated: that human life is very short. Before long all of us will be laid out side by side.

vii. That it's not what *they* do that bothers us: that's a problem for their minds, not ours. It's our own misperceptions. Discard them. Be willing to give up thinking of this as a catastrophe... and your anger is gone. How do you do that? By recognizing that you've suffered no disgrace. Unless disgrace is the only thing that can hurt you, you're doomed to commit innumerable offenses—to become a thief, or heaven only knows what else.

viii. How much more damage anger and grief do than the things that cause them.

ix. That kindness is invincible, provided it's sincere—not ironic or an act. What can even the most vicious person do if you keep treating him with kindness and gently set him straight—if you get the chance—correcting him cheerfully at the exact moment that he's trying to do you harm. "No, no, my friend. That isn't what we're here for. It isn't me who's harmed by that. It's you." And show him, gently and without pointing fingers, that it's so. That bees don't behave like this—or any other animals with a sense of community. Don't do it sardonically or meanly, but affectionately—with no hatred in your heart. And not ex cathedra or to impress third parties, but speaking directly. Even if there are other people around.

Keep these nine points in mind, like gifts from the nine Muses, and start becoming a human being. Now and for the rest of your life.

And along with not getting angry at others, try not to pander either. Both are forms of selfishness; both of them will do you harm. When you start to lose your temper, remember: There's nothing manly about rage. It's courtesy and kindness that define a human being—and a man. That's who possesses strength and nerves and guts, not the angry whiners. To react like that brings you closer to impassivity—and so to strength. Pain is the opposite of strength, and so is anger. Both are things we suffer from, and yield to.

... and one more thought, from Apollo:

x. That to expect bad people not to injure others is crazy. It's to ask the impossible. And to let them behave like that to other people but expect them to exempt you is arrogant—the act of a tyrant.

19. Four habits of thought to watch for, and erase from your mind when you catch them. Tell yourself:

- This thought is unnecessary.
- This one is destructive to the people around you.
- This wouldn't be what you really think (to say what you don't think—the definition of absurdity).

And the fourth reason for self-reproach: that the more divine part of you has been beaten and subdued by the degraded mortal part—the body and its stupid self-indulgence.

20. Your spirit and the fire contained within you are drawn by their nature upward. But they comply with the world's designs and submit to being mingled here below. And the elements of earth and water in you are drawn by their nature downward. But are forced to rise, and take up a position not their own. So even the elements obey the world—when ordered and compelled—and man their stations until the signal to abandon them arrives.

So why should your intellect be the only dissenter—the only one complaining about its posting? It's not as if anything is being forced on it. Only what its own nature requires. And yet it refuses to comply, and sets off in the opposite direction. Because to be drawn toward what is wrong and self-indulgent, toward anger and fear and pain, is to revolt against nature. And for the mind to complain about anything that happens is to desert its post. It was created to show reverence—respect for the divine—no less than to act justly. That too is an element of coexistence and a prerequisite for justice.

21. "If you don't have a consistent goal in life, you can't live it in a consistent way."

Unhelpful, unless you specify a goal.

There is no common benchmark for all the things that people think are good—except for a few, the ones that affect us all. So the goal should be a common one—a civic one. If you direct all your energies toward that, your actions will be consistent. And so will you.

22. The town mouse and the country mouse. Distress and agitation of the town mouse.

23. Socrates used to call popular beliefs "the monsters under the bed"—only useful for frightening children with.

24. At festivals the Spartans put their guests' seats in the shade, but sat themselves down anywhere.

25. Socrates declining Perdiccas's invitation "so as to avoid dying a thousand deaths" (by accepting a favor he couldn't pay back).

26. This advice from Epicurean writings: to think continually of one of the men of old who lived a virtuous life.

27. The Pythagoreans tell us to look at the stars at daybreak. To remind ourselves how they complete the tasks assigned them—always the same tasks, the same way. And their order, purity, nakedness. Stars wear no concealment.

28. Socrates dressed in a towel, the time Xanthippe took his cloak and went out. The friends who were embarrassed and avoided him when they saw him dressed like that, and what Socrates said to them.

29. Mastery of reading and writing requires a master. Still more so life.

30. "…For you/Are but a slave and have no claim to *logos*."

31. "But my heart rejoiced."

32. "And jeer at virtue with their taunts and sneers."

33. Stupidity is expecting figs in winter, or children in old age.

34. As you kiss your son good night, says Epictetus, whisper to yourself, "He may be dead in the morning."
    Don't tempt fate, you say.
    By talking about a natural event? Is fate tempted when we speak of grain being reaped?

35. Grapes.
    Unripe…ripened…then raisins.
    Constant transitions.
    Not the "not" but the "not yet."

36. "No thefts of free will reported." [—Epictetus.]

37. "We need to master the art of acquiescence. We need to pay attention to our impulses, making sure they don't go unmoderated, that they benefit others, that they're worthy of us. We need to steer clear of desire in any form and not try to avoid what's beyond our control."

38. "This is not a debate about just anything," he said, "but about sanity itself."

39. Socrates: What do you want, rational minds or irrational ones?
   —Rational ones.
   Healthy or sick?
   —Healthy.
   Then work to obtain them.
   —We already have.
   Then why all this squabbling?

BOOK 12

1. Everything you're trying to reach—by taking the long way round—you could have right now, this moment. If you'd only stop thwarting your own attempts. If you'd only let go of the past, entrust the future to Providence, and guide the present toward reverence and justice.

Reverence: so you'll accept what you're allotted. Nature intended it for you, and you for it.

Justice: so that you'll speak the truth, frankly and without evasions, and act as you should—and as other people deserve.

Don't let anything deter you: other people's misbehavior, your own misperceptions, What People Will Say, or the feelings of the body that covers you (let the affected part take care of those). And if, when it's time to depart, you shunt everything aside except your mind and the divinity within... if it isn't ceasing to live that you're afraid of but never beginning to live properly... then you'll be worthy of the world that made you.

No longer an alien in your own land.

No longer shocked by everyday events—as if they were unheard-of aberrations.

No longer at the mercy of this, or that.

2. God sees all our souls freed from their fleshly containers, stripped clean of their bark, cleansed of their grime. He grasps with his intelligence alone what was poured and channeled from himself

into them. If you learn to do the same, you can avoid a great deal of distress. When you see through the flesh that covers you, will you be unsettled by clothing, mansions, celebrity—the painted sets, the costume cupboard?

3. Your three components: body, breath, mind. Two are yours in trust; to the third alone you have clear title.

If you can cut yourself—your mind—free of what other people do and say, of what you've said or done, of the things that you're afraid will happen, the impositions of the body that contains you and the breath within, and what the whirling chaos sweeps in from outside, so that the mind is freed from fate, brought to clarity, and lives life on its own recognizance—doing what's right, accepting what happens, and speaking the truth—

If you can cut free of impressions that cling to the mind, free of the future and the past—can make yourself, as Empedocles says, "a sphere rejoicing in its perfect stillness," and concentrate on living what can be lived (which means the present)... then you can spend the time you have left in tranquillity. And in kindness. And at peace with the spirit within you.

4. It never ceases to amaze me: we all love ourselves more than other people, but care more about their opinion than our own. If a god appeared to us—or a wise human being, even—and prohibited us from concealing our thoughts or imagining anything without immediately shouting it out, we wouldn't make it through a single day. That's how much we value other people's opinions—instead of our own.

5. How is it that the gods arranged everything with such skill, such care for our well-being, and somehow overlooked one thing: that certain people—in fact, the best of them, the gods' own part-

ners, the ones whose piety and good works brought them closest to the divine—that these people, when they die, should cease to exist forever? Utterly vanished.

Well, assuming that's really true, you can be sure they would have arranged things differently, if that had been appropriate. If it were the right thing to do, they could have done it, and if it were natural, nature would have demanded it. So from the fact that they didn't—if that's the case—we can conclude that it was inappropriate.

Surely you can see yourself that to ask the question is to challenge the gods' fairness. And why would you be bringing in fairness unless the gods are, in fact, fair—and absolutely so?

And if they are, how could they have carelessly overlooked something so unfair—so illogical—in setting up the world?

6. Practice even what seems impossible.
The left hand is useless at almost everything, for lack of practice. But it guides the reins better than the right. From practice.

7. The condition of soul and body when death comes for us.
Shortness of life.
Vastness of time before and after.
Fragility of matter.

8. To see the causes of things stripped bare. The aim of actions.
Pain. Pleasure. Death. Fame.
Who is responsible for our own restlessness.
That no one obstructs us.
That it's all in how you perceive it.

9. The student as boxer, not fencer.
The fencer's weapon is picked up and put down again.
The boxer's is part of him. All he has to do is clench his fist.

10. To see things as they are. Substance, cause and purpose.

11. The freedom to do only what God wants, and accept whatever God sends us.

11a. What it's made of.

12. The gods are not to blame. They do nothing wrong, on purpose or by accident. Nor men either; they don't do it on purpose. No one is to blame.

13. The foolishness of people who are surprised by anything that happens. Like travelers amazed at foreign customs.

14. Fatal necessity, and inescapable order. Or benevolent Providence. Or confusion—random and undirected.

If it's an inescapable necessity, why resist it?

If it's Providence, and admits of being worshipped, then try to be worthy of God's aid.

If it's confusion and anarchy, then be grateful that on this raging sea you have a mind to guide you. And if the storm should carry you away, let it carry off flesh, breath and all the rest, but not the mind. Which can't be swept away.

15. The lamp shines until it is put out, without losing its gleam, and yet in you it all gutters out so early—truth, justice, self-control?

16. When someone seems to have injured you:
But how can I be sure?
And in any case, keep in mind:

- that he's already been tried and convicted—by himself. (Like scratching your own eyes out.)
- that to expect a bad person not to harm others is like expecting fig trees not to secrete juice, babies not to cry, horses not to neigh—the inevitable not to happen.

What else could they do—with that sort of character?
If you're still angry, then get to work on that.

17. If it's not right, don't do it. If it's not true, don't say it. Let your intention be < … >

18. At all times, look at the thing itself—the thing behind the appearance—and unpack it by analysis:

- cause
- substance
- purpose
- and the length of time it exists.

19. It's time you realized that you have something in you more powerful and miraculous than the things that affect you and make you dance like a puppet.

What's in my thoughts at this moment? Fear? Jealousy? Desire? Feelings like that?

20. To undertake nothing:

i. at random or without a purpose;
ii. for any reason but the common good.

21. That before long you'll be no one, and nowhere. Like all the things you see now. All the people now living.

Everything's destiny is to change, to be transformed, to perish. So that new things can be born.

22. It's all in how you perceive it. You're in control. You can dispense with misperception at will, like rounding the point. Serenity, total calm, safe anchorage.

23. A given action that stops when it's supposed to is none the worse for stopping. Nor the person engaged in it either. So too with the succession of actions we call "life." If it ends when it's supposed to, it's none the worse for that. And the person who comes to the end of the line has no cause for complaint. The time and stopping point are set by nature—our own nature, in some cases (death from old age); or nature as a whole, whose parts, shifting and changing, constantly renew the world, and keep it on schedule.

Nothing that benefits all things can be ugly or out of place. The end of life is not an evil—it doesn't disgrace us. (Why should we be ashamed of an involuntary act that injures no one?). It's a good thing—scheduled by the world, promoting it, promoted by it.

This is how we become godlike—following God's path, and reason's goals.

24. Three things, essential at all times:

i(a). your own actions: that they're not arbitrary or different from what abstract justice would do.

i(b). external events: that they happen randomly or by design. You can't complain about chance. You can't argue with Providence.

ii. what all things are like, from the planting of the seed to the quickening of life, and from its quickening to its relinquishment. Where the parts came from and where they return to.

iii. that if you were suddenly lifted up and could see life and its variety from a vast height, and at the same time all the things around you, in the sky and beyond it, you'd see how pointless it is. And no matter how often you saw it, it would be the same: the same life forms, the same life span.

Arrogance... about *this?*

25. Throw out your misperceptions and you'll be fine. (And who's stopping you from throwing them out?)

26. To be angry at something means you've forgotten:

That everything that happens is natural.
That the responsibility is theirs, not yours.

And further...

That whatever happens has always happened, and always will, and is happening at this very moment, everywhere. Just like this.
What links one human being to all humans: not blood, or birth, but mind.

And...

That an individual's mind is God and of God.
That nothing belongs to anyone. Children, body, life itself—all of them come from that same source.
That it's all how you choose to see things.
That the present is all we have to live in. Or to lose.

27. Constantly run down the list of those who felt intense anger at something: the most famous, the most unfortunate, the most hated, the most whatever. And ask: Where is all that now? Smoke, dust, leg-

end...or not even a legend. Think of all the examples: Fabius Catullinus in the country, Lusius Lupus in the orchard, Stertinius at
Baiae, Tiberius on Capri, Velius Rufus...obsession and arrogance.

And how trivial the things we want so passionately are. And
how much more philosophical it would be to take what we're given
and show uprightness, self-control, obedience to God, without
making a production of it. There's nothing more insufferable than
people who boast about their own humility.

28. People ask, "Have you ever seen the gods you worship? How
can you be sure they exist?"
Answers:

   i. Just look around you.
   ii. I've never seen my soul either. And yet I revere it.

That's how I know the gods exist and why I revere them—from having felt their power, over and over.

29. Salvation: to see each thing for what it is—its nature and its purpose.

To do only what is right, say only what is true, without holding
back.

What else could it be but to live life fully—to pay out goodness
like the rings of a chain, without the slightest gap.

30. Singular, not plural:

Sunlight. Though broken up by walls and mountains and a
thousand other things.

Substance. Though split into a thousand forms, variously shaped.

Life. Though distributed among a thousand different natures
with their individual limitations.

Intelligence. Even if it seems to be divided.

The other components—breath, matter—lack any awareness or connection to one another (yet unity and its gravitational pull embrace them too).

But intelligence is uniquely drawn toward what is akin to it, and joins with it inseparably, in shared awareness.

31. What is it you want? To keep on breathing? What about feeling? desiring? growing? ceasing to grow? using your voice? thinking? Which of them seems worth having?

But if you can do without them all, then continue to follow the *logos*, and God. To the end. To prize those other things—to grieve because death deprives us of them—is an obstacle.

32. The fraction of infinity, of that vast abyss of time, allotted to each of us. Absorbed in an instant into eternity.

The fraction of all substance, and all spirit.

The fraction of the whole earth you crawl about on.

Keep all that in mind, and don't treat anything as important except doing what your nature demands, and accepting what Nature sends you.

33. How the mind conducts itself. It all depends on that. All the rest is within its power, or beyond its control—corpses and smoke.

34. An incentive to treat death as unimportant: even people whose only morality is pain and pleasure can manage that much.

35. If you make ripeness alone your good...

If a few actions more or less, governed by the right *logos*, are merely a few more or less...

If it makes no difference whether you look at the world for this long or that long...

... then death shouldn't scare you.

36. You've lived as a citizen in a great city. Five years or a hundred— what's the difference? The laws make no distinction.

And to be sent away from it, not by a tyrant or a dishonest judge, but by Nature, who first invited you in—why is that so terrible?

Like the impresario ringing down the curtain on an actor:

"But I've only gotten through three acts...!"

Yes. This will be a drama in three acts, the length fixed by the power that directed your creation, and now directs your dissolution. Neither was yours to determine.

So make your exit with grace—the same grace shown to you.

NOTES

1.1   *My grandfather Verus:* Verus (1).

1.2   *My father:* Verus (2).

1.3   *My mother:* Lucilla.

1.4   *My great-grandfather:* Severus (1).

       To avoid the public schools: Roman aristocrats normally preferred to have their sons educated by private tutors (often specially trained household slaves) who were considered safer and more reliable than the professional schoolmasters who taught all comers for a fee.

1.5   *My first teacher:* Not named and most likely a slave.

       Not to support this side or that: Literally, "not to be a Green or a Blue; not to support the *parmularius* [a gladiator with a small shield] or the *scutarius* [who carried a larger shield]."

1.6   *the camp-bed and the cloak:* Symbols of an ascetic lifestyle. Marcus's sleeping arrangements are recorded by the *Historia Augusta:* "He used to sleep on the ground, and his mother had a hard time convincing him to sleep on a cot spread with skins."

1.7   *his own copy:* It is unclear whether this refers to Arrian's *Discourses of Epictetus* or to a set of unpublished notes, perhaps taken by Rusticus himself.

1.13 *Domitius and Athenodotus:* The anecdote Marcus refers to is unknown.

1.14 *My brother:* Probably a copyist's error based on confusion between
the names Verus and Severus.

Thrasea, Helvidius, Cato: For the significance of these three figures as
Stoic exemplars see the Introduction.

1.16 *My adopted father:* Antoninus Pius. The sketch here seems to be a
development and expansion of the briefer assessment in 6.30.

Putting a stop to the pursuit of boys: This may be meant as a critique of
Antoninus's predecessor, Hadrian (2), whose love affair with the
youth Antinoüs was notorious. Alternatively it might refer to legal
restrictions on pederasty (which was common in upper-class
Greek and Roman society), or to Antoninus's own self-restraint.

The robe . . . the customs agent's apology: These examples of Antoninus's
modesty are too compressed and allusive to be intelligible to anyone but Marcus himself.

as they say of Socrates: Marcus may be recalling a similar comment by
Xenophon, *Memorabilia* 1.3.14; Socrates' ability to drink heavily
without any apparent effect is celebrated in Plato's *Symposium*
(179c, 220a).

Maximus's illness: For Maximus see the Index of Persons; nothing is
known of his illness.

1.17 *someone:* Antoninus.

the kind of brother: Verus (3).

the honors they seemed to want: Marcus may be thinking of Herodes
Atticus and Fronto, both of whom held consulships in 143, soon
after Marcus became the heir apparent. Perhaps also of Rusticus,
who held a second consulship in 162.

I never laid a finger: Household slaves were often exposed to sexual
abuse at the hands of their owners.

That I have the wife I do: Faustina.

at Caieta: A seaport on the west coast of Italy. The Greek text adds
an unintelligible phrase, which some scholars interpret as a reference to "an oracle."

"we need the help ...": Apparently a quotation, but not from any surviving work.

2. *On the River Gran, Among the Quadi:* The notation is transmitted at the end of Book 1, but is more likely to belong here. The Gran (or Hron) is a tributary of the Danube flowing through modern-day Slovakia. The Quadi were a Suebian tribe in the Morava River valley, subdued during the Marcomannic Wars of the early 170s.

2.2 *Throw away... right now:* These words are deleted or transposed elsewhere by some editors.

2.10 *the ones committed out of desire are worse:* Strictly speaking, this assessment is in conflict with Stoic doctrine, which holds that there are no degrees of wrongness; all wrong actions are equally wrong and it makes no sense to speak of one as being "worse" than another.

2.13 *"delving into...":* A line from the lyric poet Pindar (frg. 282), quoted also by Plato, *Theaetetus* 173e.

3. *In Carnuntum:* Transmitted at the end of Book 2, but probably meant to head Book 3. Carnuntum was a fortress on the Danube which housed the Legio XIV Gemina and served as the seat of the governor of Upper Pannonia. Marcus is known to have been in the area in 172 and 173.

3.3 *Chaldaeans:* The Chaldaeans (Babylonians) had a special reputation as astrologers.
    Democritus: Apparently an error for another pre-Socratic philosopher, Pherecydes, who was said to have been eaten by worms. (Democritus's name was often coupled with that of Heraclitus, which may explain Marcus's slip here.)
    Socrates: The "vermin" who killed Socrates are the Athenians who prosecuted and condemned him.

3.6 *as Socrates used to say:* It is not clear whether Marcus is alluding to a specific passage (perhaps Plato, *Phaedo* 83a–b) or merely to a general impression of Socratic doctrine.

3.14 *your* Brief Comments: Evidently collections of anecdotes and/or quotations put together by Marcus himself for his own use, like parts of the extant *Meditations.*

3.15 *They don't realize...:* The significance of this entry (particularly the last phrase) is unclear.

3.16 *people who do < ...>:* It seems clear that something is missing from the text, perhaps deliberately omitted by a prudish copyist.

4.3 *to ward off all < ...>:* The missing word must be something like "anxiety."

"The world is nothing but change...": Democritus frg. B 115.

4.18 *< ...> not to be distracted:* The text as transmitted includes the words "good," "black character," and "suspicion," but no coherent sense can be made of them.

4.19 *You're out of step...:* The text of this sentence is disturbed and the translation correspondingly uncertain.

4.23 *The poet:* Aristophanes frg. 112.

4.24 *"If you seek tranquillity..."*: Democritus frg. B 3.

4.30 *A philosopher without clothes...:* If the text is sound it is not easy to interpret convincingly. The rendering here (which differs from most previous versions) represents my best guess at the sense, but is far from certain.

4.33 *Camillus, Caeso, Volesus, Dentatus:* Heroes of the Roman Republic (see the Index of Persons). Only Camillus was well known; the others may have been purposely chosen for their obscurity.

"unknown, unasked-for": Homer, *Odyssey* 1.242.

4.41 *"A little wisp of soul..."*: Epictetus frg. 26 (presumably from one of the lost books of the *Discourses*).

4.46 *"When earth dies..."*: Heraclitus frg. B 76.

"Those who have forgotten...": idem. frg. B 71.

"They are at odds...": idem. frg. B 72.

"they find alien...": idem. frg. B 73.

"Our words and actions...": idem. frg. B 74.

4.48 *Helike, Pompeii, Herculaneum:* Helike was a Greek city destroyed by an earthquake and tidal wave in 373 B.C. Pompeii and its neighbor city Herculaneum were destroyed by the eruption of Mount Vesuvius in A.D. 79.

4.49a   *It's unfortunate:* It has been plausibly suggested that this entry is a quotation from a lost section of Epictetus's *Discourses.*

4.50   *Caedicianus, Fabius, Julian, Lepidus:* With the possible exception of Caedicianus and Lepidus (see the Index of Persons), none of these figures can be identified.

5.8   *"the doctor":* Literally, "Asclepius." Patients sleeping in his temple sometimes had dream visions of the god and received suggestions for treatment from him. But the name might simply indicate a human physician.

5.10   *a pervert:* The Greek word (used also in 6.34) is a contemptuous term referring to the passive partner in homosexual intercourse; it has no exact English equivalent ("pervert," although overly broad, at least has the right tone). Marcus is probably using it as a generalized term of abuse.

5.12   *"so many goods ...":* Proverbial: the rich man owns "so many goods he has no place to shit." The saying is at least as old as the fourth-century B.C. comic poet Menander, who quotes it in the surviving fragments of his play *The Apparition.*

5.29   *If the smoke makes me cough:* The metaphor is drawn from Epictetus, *Discourses* 1.25.18.

5.31   *"wrong and unworthy ...":* Homer, *Odyssey* 4.690.

5.33   *"gone from the earth ...":* Hesiod, *Works and Days* 197.

5.36   *Not to be overwhelmed:* The remainder of this book is unintelligible in places, perhaps because the end of the original papyrus roll suffered accidental damage. I have divided the text into three separate sections, but without great confidence that this is correct.
        Like the old man: The reference is obscure. A scene from a lost tragedy?

6.13   *Crates on Xenocrates:* The meaning of this reference is unknown.

6.30   *Take Antoninus as your model:* The sketch that follows seems to be a preliminary version of the longer portrait at 1.16.

6.34   *perverts:* See 5.10 note.

6.42   *"those who sleep ...":* Heraclitus frg. B 75.

   the bad line in the play: Chrysippus frg. 1181 (= Plutarch, *On Stoic Self-Contradictions* 13f.). Chrysippus compared the existence of evil to a deliberately bathetic line in a comedy—bad in itself, but an essential part of a good play.

7.12 *not:* The transmitted text reads "or," but this can hardly be correct (compare 3.5).

7.15 *Like gold or emerald or purple:* Compare Epictetus, *Discourses* 1.2.17–18: "You see yourself as one thread in a garment... But I want to be the purple thread, the small, glistening one that enhances the others."

7.24 †... † *or in the end is put out:* I have omitted a short phrase from which it is impossible to extract any meaning.

7.31a *"... all are relative...":* A paraphrase of Democritus frg. B 9, in which qualities like sweetness or bitterness are said to be "relative" or "conventional" rather than inherent (what tastes sweet to one person may be bitter to another). Marcus apparently sees the observation as compatible with the Stoic doctrine that "it's all in how you perceive it" (12.8), though he naturally rejects the subsequent reference to atoms. The final phrase is corrupt beyond repair.

7.32 *[On death]:* The headings of this and the next two entries are probably not Marcus's own, but additions by a later reader.

7.35 *"If his mind is filled...":* Plato, *Republic* 6.486a.

7.36 *"Kingship...":* Antisthenes frg. 20b (also quoted by Epictetus, *Discourses* 4.6.20).

7.38 *"And why should we feel anger...":* Euripides, frg. 287 (from the lost *Bellerophon* quoted also at 11.6).

7.39 *"May you bring joy...":* Source unknown; perhaps from a lost epic.

7.40 *"To harvest life...":* Euripides, frg. 757 (from the lost *Hypsipyle*).

7.41 *"If I and my two children...":* Euripides, frg. 208 (from the lost *Antiope;* quoted also at 11.6).

7.42 *"For what is just and good...":* Ibid., frg. 918 (from an unknown play).

7.43 *No chorus of lamentation:* This might be a quotation, like the preceding entries, but if so, we do not know its source.

7.44 *"Then the only proper response...":* Plato, *Apology* 28b.

7.45   *"It's like this…"*: Ibid., 28d.

7.46   *"But, my good friend…"*: Plato, *Gorgias* 512d.

7.48   *[Plato has it right]:* The passage that follows does not correspond to anything in Plato's preserved writings, and it seems likely that the phrase was inserted by a later reader who mistook it for a quotation.

7.50   *"Earth's offspring…"*: Euripides, frg. 839 (from the lost *Chrysippus*).

7.51   *"… with food and drink…"*: Euripides, *Suppliants* 1110–1111.

7.51a *"To labor cheerfully…"*: From an unknown tragedy.

7.63   *"Against our will…"*: Epictetus, *Discourses* 1.28.4 (also 2.22.37), paraphrasing Plato, *Sophist* 228c.

7.64   *what Epicurus said:* Epicurus frg. 447.

7.66   *by spending the night out in the cold:* This anecdote is told by Alcibiades in Plato's *Symposium* (220).

       the man from Salamis: During the brief reign of the "Thirty Tyrants" at Athens, Socrates was ordered to collaborate with the regime by arresting a certain Leon, but refused; the story is told in Plato's *Apology* (32c).

       "swaggered about the streets": A line from Aristophanes' comedy *Clouds* (362), which pokes fun at Socrates.

8.25   *Verus … Lucilla:* Marcus's parents.

       Hadrian: Most likely this refers to the rhetorician (Hadrian 1) rather than the emperor (Hadrian 2).

8.35   *We have various abilities…:* The text here appears to be corrupt and the translation is necessarily uncertain.

8.38   *Look at it clearly:* The text, meaning and articulation of entries 38 and 39 are very uncertain. Earlier editors printed the opening of 38 as the end of 37, and took the phrases "Look at it clearly—if you can" and "To the best of my judgment" as a single unit, though the resulting sentence yields no coherent sense. I follow J. Dalfen in separating them.

8.39   *"To the best of my judgment…":* I have placed the entry in quotation marks on the basis of the opening phrase, which includes a parenthetical "he [or "someone"] says." This assumes that the phrase is correctly transmitted (it is certainly not easy to construe), and that it should be taken with what follows rather than what precedes, which is far from certain (see previous note). However, the entry as a whole (an implicit criticism of the Epicureans' view of pleasure as the supreme good) does not strike me as being typical of Marcus's style, and I suspect he may indeed be quoting some earlier writer.

8.41   *"a sphere…":* Empedocles frg. B27, quoted in fuller form at 12.3.

8.57   *Its beams get their name…:* This (false) derivation is a typical example of ancient etymology, a science in which the early Stoics were much interested.

9.2   *the "next best voyage":* A proverbial phrase meaning having to row when one cannot sail.

9.24   *"Odysseus in the Underworld":* The reference is to Book 11 of the *Odyssey,* in which Odysseus descends to Hades and encounters the shades of his companions who died at Troy.

9.29   *Demetrius of Phalerum:* It has been suggested that "of Phalerum" is a later reader's (mistaken) addition, and that Marcus had in mind the Hellenistic monarch Demetrius Poliorcetes ("the city-sacker"). But there seems no reason to doubt the transmitted text.

9.41   *"During my illness…":* Epicurus frg. 191.

10.10   *Sarmatians:* One of the barbarian tribes Marcus spent his last decade fighting.

10.21   *"The earth knows longing…":* Euripides frg. 898.

10.23   *"fencing a sheepfold…":* A paraphrase of Plato, *Theaetetus* 174d, in which we are told that the philosopher will look down on a king as if the latter were a humble shepherd.

10.31   *When you look…:* Most of the names mentioned here are mere ciphers (see the Index of Persons for the best guess as to their identities), but Marcus's point does not depend on knowledge of the individuals.

10.33   *as a cylinder rolls down:* The comparison is taken from Chrysippus frg. 1000.

10.34 "... *leaves that the wind*...": Homer, *Iliad* 6.147 ff., a very famous passage.

11.3 *[like the Christians]:* This ungrammatical phrase is almost certainly a marginal comment by a later reader; there is no reason to think Marcus had the Christians in mind here. (See Introduction.)

11.6 *"o Mount Cithaeron!":* Sophocles, *Oedipus the King* 1391 (Oedipus's anguished cry after blinding himself, invoking the mountain he was abandoned on as a baby.)

"*If I and my two children*...": See on 7.41.

"*And why should we feel anger...?":* See on 7.38.

"*To harvest life*...": See on 7.40.

11.18 *from Apollo:* Often depicted as the leader of the nine Muses.

11.22 *The town mouse:* Aesop, *Fables* 297. The significance of the allusion is unclear.

11.23 *"the monsters under the bed":* Plato, *Crito* 46c and *Phaedo* 77e; Marcus is probably drawing on Epictetus, *Discourses* 2.1.14.

11.25 *Perdiccas's invitation:* In fact the ruler who invited Socrates to his court was Perdiccas's successor Archelaus (resigned 413–399).

11.26 *This advice:* Epicurus frg. 210.

11.28 *Socrates dressed in a towel:* The anecdote is not preserved.

11.30 *"For you/Are but a slave*...": From a lost tragedy. Marcus twists what must have been the sense of the original ("it is not for you to speak") by taking *logos* in its broader, philosophical sense.

11.31 *"But my heart rejoiced":* Homer, *Odyssey* 9.413.

11.32 *"And jeer at virtue*...": Hesiod, *Works and Days* 186, but "virtue" is Marcus's substitution. Hesiod has "and jeer at them," in a completely different context.

11.33 *Stupidity is expecting figs:* A paraphrase of Epictetus, *Discourses* 3.24.86.

11.34 *As you kiss your son:* Ibid., 3.24.88.

11.36 *"No thefts of free will*...": Ibid., 3.22.105 (the attribution in the text is probably an addition by a later reader who recognized the quotation).

11.37 *"We need to master*...": Ibid., frg. 27.

11.38 *"This is not a debate…":* Ibid., frg. 28.

11.39 *Socrates: What do you want?* Source uncertain: perhaps from a lost section of Epictetus.

12.3   *"a sphere rejoicing…":* Empedocles frg. B 27 (also quoted at 8.41).

12.11a *What it's made of:* Part of 12 in the manuscripts; placed in 11 by Meric Casaubon. Perhaps an incomplete entry, perhaps an addition by a later hand.

12.17 *Let your intention be< … >:* The division between Chapters 17 and 18 is unclear, and it seems likely that some text has been lost.

12.27 *Fabius Catullinus et al.:* Most of the references are obscure; see the Index of Persons for what can be guessed of them.

12.34 *people whose only morality…:* The Epicureans.

INDEX OF PERSONS

This list covers only persons named, referred to, or quoted in the text of the *Meditations* itself.

AGRIPPA: Roman general; adviser and close associate of AUGUSTUS, whose daughter he married. (8.31)

ALCIPHRON: Not certainly identified, although the context makes it clear that he must be a contemporary of Marcus's. He might be the Alciphron who authored a surviving collection of imaginary letters from courtesans, fishermen, etc., or a philosopher from Magnesia on the Maeander, quoted twice by the third-century antiquarian Athenaeus. (10.31)

ALEXANDER (1) "THE LITERARY CRITIC": A Greek from Cotiaeum in Syria, teacher of the great orator Aelius Aristides, as well as Marcus. (1.10)

ALEXANDER (2) "THE PLATONIST": A literary figure, mockingly dubbed Alexander Peloplaton ("The Play-Doh Plato") by his rivals. He served as head of the Greek side of the imperial secretariat. (1.12)

ALEXANDER (3) "THE GREAT": (356–323 B.C.), ruler of Macedon (336–323) who conquered much of the Near and Middle East before dying at the age of thirty-three. His career was a favorite topic for moralizers and rhetoricians. (3.3, 6.24, 8.3, 9.29, 10.27)

ANTISTHENES: Follower of SOCRATES and forerunner of the Cynic school (quoted 7.36).

ANTONINUS: Titus Aurelius Antoninus Pius, Roman emperor (138–161). He adopted Marcus in 138 at the age of sixteen (1.16, 1.17, 4.33, 6.30, 8.25, 9.21, 10.27). Marcus also refers to himself by this name (6.44).

APOLLONIUS: Apollonius of Chalcedon, Stoic philosopher and one of Marcus's teachers. (1.8, 1.17)

ARCHIMEDES: Mathematician, scientist and engineer (c. 287–212 B.C.) from the Greek city of Syracuse in Sicily, known especially for his work on hydrostatics. (6.47)

AREIUS: Stoic philosopher prominent at the court of AUGUSTUS. (8.31)

ARISTOPHANES: Athenian comic playwright (c. 455–c. 386 B.C.). Eleven of his approximately forty comedies survive, and are characterized by fantastic plots, scatological dialogue, outrageous political satire, and elegant choral songs. (quoted 4.23, 7.66)

ASCLEPIUS: Greek god of medicine. (6.43; compare 5.8 and note)

ATHENODOTUS: A Stoic philosopher and teacher of FRONTO. (1.13)

AUGUSTUS: (63 B.C.–A.D. 14). Born Gaius Octaviaus, great-nephew and adopted son of Julius CAESAR. He attained power following Caesar's assassination and became sole ruler of the Roman world after defeating Caesar's lieutenant Marcus Antonius at the battle of Actium in 31 B.C. Through his lieutenants AGRIPPA and MAECENAS he was responsible for major civic improvements and an active program of literary and artistic patronage. (4.33, 8.5, 8.31)

BACCHEIUS: Platonic philosopher. (1.6)

BENEDICTA: Unknown, but she and THEODOTUS were most likely household slaves. (1.17)

BRUTUS: Marcus Junius Brutus (85–42 B.C.), Roman aristocrat and politician who led the conspiracy to assassinate Julius CAESAR in 44 B.C. and committed suicide when the battle of Philippi ended hopes of restoring the Republic. (1.14)

CAEDICIANUS: Perhaps identical with a governor of Dacia in the 120s and 130s. (4.50)

CAESAR: Gaius Julius Caesar (100–44 B.C.), Roman politician and general who marched on Rome in 49 B.C., precipitating a civil war against forces loyal to POMPEY and the Senate. After the defeat of the Republican forces at the battle of Pharsalia and the murder of Pompey he was made dictator for life, but assassinated in 44 B.C. (3.3, 8.3)

CAESO: Unknown, though obviously a figure from Republican history. (4.33)

CAMILLUS: Marcus Furius Camillus, the (perhaps mythical) fourth-century B.C. general who saved Rome when it was under attack by invading Gauls. (4.33)

CATO (1): Marcus Porcius Cato "the Elder," consul and censor in the second century B.C.; author of a surviving work on agriculture and a lost history. He was an emblem of Roman moral rectitude and rough virtue. (4.33)

CATO (2): Marcus Porcius Cato "the Younger" (95–46 B.C.), great-grandson of Cato (1), a senator and well-known Stoic in the late Republic. He fought on the Republican side against Julius CAESAR and committed suicide after the battle of Thapsus. He was immortalized in the poet Lucan's epic *The Civil War*, and became an emblem of Stoic resistance to tyranny. (1.14)

CATULUS: Cinna Catulus is named, along with MAXIMUS, as a Stoic mentor of Marcus's by the *Historia Augusta*, but nothing else is known of him. (1.13)

CECROPS: Legendary founder of Athens. (4.23)

CELER: Rhetorician who taught both Marcus and Lucius VERUS. (8.25)

CHABRIAS: Evidently an associate of HADRIAN (2), like DIOTIMUS, but not otherwise known. (8.37)

CHARAX: Perhaps Charax of Pergamum, a historian known from other sources to have been active in the second or third century. (8.25)

CHRYSIPPUS: Stoic philosopher (280–207 B.C.), succeeded Zeno and Cleanthes as leader of the school. His writings laid out the fundamental doctrines of early Stoicism. (6.42, 7.19)

CLOTHO: One of the three Fates of Greek mythology who are imagined as spinning or weaving human fortunes. (4.34)

CRATES: Cynic philosopher (c. 365–285 B.C.) and disciple of DIOGENES. (6.13)

CRITO: Most likely the physician Titus Statilius Crito, active under Trajan. (10.31)

CROESUS: Sixth-century king of Lydia, famous for his wealth and power until his kingdom fell to the Persians. (10.27)

DEMETER: Greek goddess of agriculture. (6.43)

DEMETRIUS (1) OF PHALERUM: Fourth-century B.C. philosopher, student of THEOPHRASTUS and governor of Athens under Macedonian rule. (9.29)

DEMETRIUS (2) THE PLATONIST: Probably not Demetrius (1), who was an adherent of the Peripatetic school, not a Platonist. A Cynic philosopher banished by VESPASIAN has also been suggested, but the reference is more likely to a contemporary figure now unknown. (8.25)

DEMOCRITUS: Pre-Socratic philosopher (c. 460–370 B.C.) best known for developing the theory of atoms later adopted by the Epicureans. (3.3; quoted 4.3, 4.24, 7.31a)

DENTATUS: Manius Curius Dentatus, third-century B.C. Roman general. (4.33)

DIOGENES: Greek philosopher (c. 400–c. 325 B.C.) and founder of the Cynic school, notable for his extreme ascetic lifestyle and contempt for social conventions. (8.3, 11.6)

DIOGNETUS: Marcus's drawing teacher (according to the *Historia Augusta*), though the entry suggests that he played a greater role in Marcus's development than this might suggest. (1.6)

DION: Sicilian aristocrat, a protégé of Plato, who saw in him a potential philosopher-king. (1.14)

DIOTIMUS: Evidently an associate of HADRIAN (2), not otherwise known. (8.25, 8.37)

DOMITIUS: Unidentified, perhaps a student of ATHENODOTUS. (1.13)

FABIUS CATULLINUS: Unknown. Perhaps to be identified with the FABIUS of 4.50. (12.27)

FAUSTINA: Wife of ANTONINUS Pius (8.25). Marcus married their daughter, also Faustina (1.17).

FRONTO: Marcus Cornelius Fronto (c. 95–c. 166), rhetorician from Cirta in North Africa, and a key figure in Marcus's education. Portions of his letters to Marcus survive in two palimpsest manuscripts discovered in the early nineteenth century. (1.11)

HADRIAN (1): Prominent rhetorician; no relation to the emperor. (8.25)

HADRIAN (2): Roman emperor (117–138), best known for his travels and cultural interests; adopted ANTONINUS as his heir on the condition that the latter adopt Marcus and Lucius VERUS. (4.33, 8.5, 8.37, 10.27)

HELVIDIUS: Helvidius Priscus (died c. 75), son-in-law of THRASEA Paetus, exiled and later executed for his opposition to the emperor VESPASIAN. (1.14)

HERACLITUS: Pre-Socratic philosopher (active c. 500 B.C.) from the city of Ephesus, famous for his cryptic and paradoxical utterances. His exaltation of the *logos* as a cosmic power and his identification of fire as the primal substance were important influences on the Stoics (see also Introduction). According to the third-century A.D. biographer Diogenes Laertius, he died of dropsy, which he tried to cure by immersing himself in manure; this account is almost certainly a later fiction. (3.3, 6.47, 8.3; quoted or paraphrased 4.46, 6.42)

HIPPARCHUS: Second-century B.C. Greek astronomer. (6.47)

HIPPOCRATES: Greek doctor active in the fifth century B.C.; various medical writings are transmitted under his name, as is the Hippocratic Oath still administered to doctors. (3.3)

HYMEN: Unknown; the comparison with SATYRON does not help identify him. (10.31)

JULIAN: This may be a friend of FRONTO's, Claudius Julianus, a proconsul of Asia at about this period. (4.50)

LEPIDUS: This might perhaps be the Roman aristocrat who briefly shared power with Marcus Antonius and the future emperor AUGUSTUS, but the context suggests an older contemporary of Marcus's. (4.50)

LUCILLA: Marcus's mother (d. 155/161). (1.3, 1.17, 8.25, 9.21)

LUSIUS LUPUS: Unknown. (12.27)

MAECENAS: Adviser and unofficial minister of culture to AUGUSTUS; patron of the poets Vergil and Horace, among others. (8.31)

MARCIANUS: Unknown philosopher. (1.6)

MAXIMUS: Claudius Maximus. Roman consul in the early 140s. Governor of Upper Pannonia in the early 150s. Later in that decade he governed North Africa, where he served as judge in the trial of the novelist Apuleius for sorcery. (1.15, 1.16, 1.17, 8.25)

MENIPPUS: Cynic philosopher (early third century B.C.) from Gadara in Syria. He features as a character in many of the satirical dialogues of Lucian. (6.47)

MONIMUS: Fourth-century B.C. Cynic philosopher and student of DIOGENES. (2.15)

NERO: Roman emperor (54–68); his name was a byword for tyranny and cruelty. (3.16)

ORIGANION: Unknown; most likely an imperial slave or freedman. (6.47)

PANTHEIA: Mistress of Lucius VERUS, mentioned in several works by the satirist Lucian. (8.37)

PERDICCAS: King of Macedon (c. 450–413 B.C.). (11.25)

PERGAMOS: Evidently an associate of Lucius VERUS, perhaps a slave or lover. (8.37)

PHALARIS: Sixth-century B.C. dictator of Agrigento in Sicily, notorious for his cruelty. (3.16)

PHILIP: King of Macedon (359–336 B.C.) and father of ALEXANDER THE GREAT. (9.29, 10.27)

PHILISTION: Unknown, most likely an imperial slave or freedman, though a contemporary mime writer of this name is also known. (6.47)

PHOCION: Athenian general and statesman of the fourth century B.C. He was eventually sentenced to death for treason, and before his execution supposedly asked his son to forgive the Athenians for condemning him. (11.13)

PHOEBUS: Unknown, most likely an imperial slave or freedman. (6.47)

PLATO: Athenian philosopher (c. 429–347 B.C.), disciple of SOCRATES and author of philosophical dialogues in which the latter is portrayed debating with his disciples and other contemporary figures. The most famous of these is perhaps the *Republic,* in which he envisions an ideal society. (7.48, 9.29, 10.23; quoted 7.44–46)

POMPEY: Gnaeus Pompeius Magnus (106–48 B.C.), Roman politician and general who rose to power in the 60s on the basis of a series of successful campaigns in the East. His brief political alliance with Julius CAESAR gave way to mutual rivalry and suspicion. When Caesar's march on Rome precipitated civil war in 49, Pompey led the senatorial resistance. Following his defeat at the battle of Pharsalus, he fled to Egypt, where he was murdered. (3.3, 8.3; family 8.31)

PYTHAGORAS: Greek mathematician, philosopher, and mystic of the late sixth century B.C. He founded a religious community in southern Italy whose members were known especially for their devotion to music and geometry. (6.47; compare 11.27)

RUSTICUS: Quintus Junius Rusticus, twice consul and city prefect of Rome in the mid-160s. His influence on Marcus is attested by the *Historia Augusta,* although the reference to him in 1.17 suggests that their relationship had its ups and downs. (1.7, 1.17)

SATYRON: Unknown, though evidently a contemporary of Marcus. (10.31)

SCIPIO: Either Publius Cornelius Scipio Africanus (c. 235–183 B.C.), who defeated Hannibal in the Second Punic War, or his grandson by

THEODOTUS: Unknown, but he and BENEDICTA were most likely household slaves. (1.17)

THEOPHRASTUS: Philosopher (c. 371–c. 287 B.C.) who succeeded Aristotle as head of the Peripatetic school. (2.10)

THRASEA: Publius Clodius Thrasea Paetus (d. 66), Roman aristocrat (consul 56) and father-in-law of HELVIDIUS Priscus. His opposition to the regime of NERO (by whom he was eventually forced to commit suicide) was informed by Stoic philosophy and in particular by the example of the younger CATO (2), of whom he wrote a biography. (1.14)

TIBERIUS: Roman emperor (14–37) who succeeded AUGUSTUS. Late in his reign he withdrew to a private estate on the island of Capri; his alleged excesses there are recorded in the biography of him by Suetonius. (12.27)

TRAJAN: Marcus Ulpius Traianus, Roman general and emperor (98–117). (4.32)

TROPAEOPHORUS: Perhaps a contemporary senator named in an inscription from Perinthus. (10.31)

VELIUS RUFUS: Addressee of one of FRONTO's letters, but otherwise unknown. (12.27)

VERUS (1): Marcus Annius Verus (d. 138), grandfather of Marcus. He was three times consul (the last two in 121 and 126); he also served as city prefect of Rome about this time. After the death of his wife he evidently took a concubine who helped raise Marcus. (1.1, 1.17, 9.21)

VERUS (2): Marcus Annius Verus, father of Marcus and husband of LUCILLA. He died sometime between 130 and 135. (1.2, 8.25)

VERUS (3): Lucius Aurelius Verus (130–169), son of HADRIAN (2)'s intended successor, Lucius Aelius. Originally named Lucius Ceionius Commodus, he was adopted along with Marcus by Antoninus Pius and on Antoninus's death became co-emperor with Marcus. He was entrusted with the conduct of the Parthian War, and campaigned with Marcus on the northern frontier before his sudden death on the way back to Rome. (1.17, 8.37)

VESPASIAN: Roman emperor (69–79). His reign represented a period of stability after the power struggle that followed the death of NERO, but he came into conflict with some members of the senatorial class, notably the Stoic HELVIDIUS Priscus. (4.32)

VOLESUS: Traditional surname in the Valerius clan, which produced a number of figures prominent in early historical accounts. Which one Marcus has in mind is uncertain. (4.33)

XANTHIPPE: Wife of SOCRATES and proverbially a shrew. (11.28)

XENOCRATES: Platonic philosopher and head of the Academy at the end of the fourth century B.C. (6.13)

XENOPHON: Probably a contemporary doctor mentioned by Galen. (10.31)

ZEUS: Sky god and head of the Greek pantheon; Marcus refers to him only rarely and normally prefers a vaguer formulation such as "God" or "the gods." (4.23, 5.7, 5.8, 11.8)

About the Translator

Gregory Hays is assistant professor of classics at the University of Virginia. He has published articles and reviews on various ancient writers and is currently completing a translation and critical study of the mythographer Fulgentius.

A Note on the Type

The principal text of this Modern Library edition was set in a digitized version of Janson, a typeface that dates from about 1690 and was cut by Nicholas Kis, a Hungarian working in Amsterdam. The original matrices have survived and are held by the Stempel foundry in Germany. Hermann Zapf redesigned some of the weights and sizes for Stempel, basing his revisions on the original design.